MW00333415

OUR VOICES RISING

One CEO's Journey to Alleviate Poverty
Using Fashion as a
Force for Good

OUR VOICES RISING

GRETCHEN HUIJSKENS

CO-FOUNDER & CEO OF TRADES OF HOPE

written collaboratively with Beth Graybill

PUNCHLINE
PUBLISHERS

Our Voices Rising

© 2023 by Gretchen Huijskens

Written collaboratively with Beth Graybill of bethgraybill.com

Requests for information should be emailed to:

info@tradesofhope.com

ISBN 978-1-955051-26-2 (softcover)

ISBN 978-1-955051-18-7 (ebook)

Any internet addresses (websites, blogs, etc.) and telephone numbers in this book are offered as a resource. They are not intended in any way to be or imply an endorsement by Gretchen Huijskens or Trades of Hope, nor does Gretchen Huijskens or Trades of Hope vouch for the content of these sites and numbers for the life of this book. All rights reserved. No portion of this book may be reproduced, stored in a retrieval system, or transmitted in any form or by any means—electronic, mechanical, photocopy, recording, scanning, or other—except for brief quotations in critical reviews or articles, without the prior written permission of the publisher.

Trades of Hope and Fashion as a Force for Good are registered trademarks of Trades of Hope LLC.

Disclaimer: Some names and identifying details have been changed to protect people's privacy. All stories are told to the best of the author's ability based on personal memories, experiences and interviewing others.

The Artisan stories and quotes were given with consent to be printed.

Gretchen Huijskens' titles may be purchased in bulk. For information, please email info@tradesofhope.com.

Cover and Interior design: Erik M. Peterson

Cover photo: Elisabeth Huijskens

Published by Punchline Publishers www.punchlineagency.com

First Printing 2023 / Printed in the United States of America

To all women who find joy
in seeing other women rise.

To my husband, Frits;
my children, Elisabeth, Harrison, and Mia;
my granddaughter, Kira & my mom, Jane.
I am who I am because of you.

Contents

· · · · · · · · · ·

Author's Note

....

WHILE THIS BOOK tells my personal story of bringing women together to alleviate poverty, I was never alone on this journey. My husband Frits has been not only emotionally and financially supportive but has always lent his attention to detail and business knowledge to my ideas. His reputation as an extremely blunt Dutchman holds true, but he is generous, huge-hearted, and sentimental. He helps my ideas come to life and loves me well. I'm so grateful.

Trades of Hope would not be what it is today without our friends, Holly Wehde and Chelsie Antos, who co-founded and helped run Trades of Hope with Elisabeth and me for the first eight years. They have moved on to other ventures and seasons of life, but we had a blast brainstorming, creating, and working closely for many years. Holly and Chelsie's work regarding culture and visionary impact are still very much a part of Trades of Hope today.

One of the biggest gifts Trades of Hope has given me is to work alongside my daughter, Elisabeth Huijskens, each day. I've watched her grow from a hardworking, creative teenager to a polished and extremely talented woman. It is her vision for the company's brand, experience, and messaging that makes Trades of Hope such a well-positioned company. And even more important is her heart for the mission of this company. She leads the team with passion and genuine love, dedicating her life to helping other women succeed. I'm thrilled that Elisabeth values education and completed her master's degree in Strategic Communications for Social Change years ago, but it is her intense 12+ years of on-the-job experience paired with her education that has made her the incredible professional woman she is today. One day, Elisabeth will lead this company better than her mom ever did, and I will be so proud.

MAMMA MIA

I ALWAYS KNEW I would adopt a child one day. Growing up and seeing commercials on television about starving children in Africa stirred something deep in my seven-year-old soul that I just couldn't shake. It made me wonder why women in the US gave birth when there were plenty of babies around the world who needed food and loving homes. Fast-forward almost twenty years. I was a young mom of two, living in Southern California while my husband traveled the world as an SAP Consultant. Elisabeth was eight and Harrison was four when we brought Mia home. Mia was just over two and a half years old. She had a tiny body but a large, loving personality.

Our journey to adopt in Haiti was eye-opening, to say the least. There were orphanages selling babies outright for profit and orphanages where the people in charge were taking more than their fair share. In fact, one orphanage was run by a local pastor who channeled funds to her personal account while kids went hungry in her "care." And then there were orphanages like the Mother Teresa orphanage operating with the best of intentions—where women genuinely cared for the children and worked so hard with so little. I visited this particular orphanage on my initial trip to Haiti. After several false starts for adoption, I had been to a multitude of places—from a hospital to several private orphanages—and saw the desperate need for quality childcare, particularly for infants and malnourished babies. There were orphanages caring for infants, it's just that there were more babies in need of care than there were beds in Port-au-Prince. And there wasn't a person with a beating heart, including every Haitian and outsider like me, who didn't want these babies to have the nourishment and one-on-one care that every baby should have when they come into this world.

In 2002, after a series of experiences and events, we started Three Angels Orphanage. If you're anti-orphanage or have experienced the trauma of living in an orphanage, *stay with me*. This isn't where the story ends.

When we first opened the orphanage for abandoned infants and babies, we had no idea what we were getting into, only that we wanted to do our best to support a community in need. And there was *a lot* of need in Port-au-Prince. I didn't know how to run an orphanage, but I knew how to take care of babies, so that's what got us started. We learned a lot of hard and good lessons along the way.

The biggest lesson learned was that many orphans around the world, including in Haiti, are not truly orphans. They're *poverty orphans*. They have parents who love them and want to continue being their parents, but they don't have the means to feed them, keep them healthy, or meet their most basic needs. This means women all over the world are dropping their children off on the doorsteps of orphanages and children's homes, forced to abandon their own babies simply because they don't have what they need to take care of them. If a mother wants her kids to survive, she gives them up so they can live with adoptive families who have the means to provide food and a safe home. On the one hand, it seems loving and humanitarian to give a child the food and shelter they need. But on the other hand, it's heartbreaking to know these babies don't get that food or shelter with their own families.

This discovery led to a lot of questions and ethical issues in my mind. And I started to wonder if charity as a whole was just a bandaid for bad situations, like the issue of poverty orphans in Haiti. Don't get me wrong, there are a lot of good and beautiful things that come out of caring for children who might not have a fighting chance of survival in their own homes. Abandoned children who are left behind at no fault of their own need help and care, too. But, when a child had a living, loving relative, adoption became a moral gray area for me. I truly believe that if those mothers had an opportunity to provide for their children, they would have done so. They want what we want for our children—to provide a safe and loving home, keep them warm, keep them fed, educate them, and make sure they have opportunities to grow up and be happy, loving adults. Unfortunately, this isn't always an option for families in underdeveloped circumstances, like so many of the women I met in Haiti.

We ran the orphanage in Haiti for eight years, and during that time, we opened a school and a medical clinic. The orphanage, school, and clinic are part of Three Angels Children's Relief to this day. They're still doing great things, just not the things I felt called to do after seeing what I saw. Once I knew that most orphans around the world are poverty orphans with living family members, I couldn't "unknow" that fact. And it changed everything for me.

But opening an orphanage in Haiti was how I met our daughter Mia.

On May 1, 2003, I traveled back to Haiti to get the orphanage up and running with a few Haitian partners we had on the ground. One of them called before I arrived to say, "I have your daughter!" Maxon knew we were planning to adopt and had already witnessed our heartbreak over one failed adoption. I'll never forget the moment one of the nannies working with us walked through the door holding a beautiful, tiny eighteen-month-old girl. Her name was Thaicha. Later we would make Thaicha her middle name and call her Mia, a decision I question to this day. I was introduced to the nanny, Madame Dauphin. We said hello to each other, and she said to Mia, "This is your Mamma!" Mia went straight into my arms, wrapped her little arms around my neck, and barely let go for the next five days. The adoption process would take another thirteen months. But I knew the moment I first held Mia that she had a piece of my heart. We now had a second daughter. Even though I had to return home to California, I would visit Mia in Haiti every few weeks. And I was now Mamma Mia, as my Haitian friends loved to say.

Mia changed the trajectory of our lives. And so did our orphanage experience in Haiti.

I couldn't keep accepting babies into our care at Three Angels, knowing most of them had loving mothers, fathers, aunts, or grandmothers who simply couldn't afford their care. As a mother to three children of my own—Elisabeth, Harrison, and now Mia—I had a burden for these women and desperately wanted to help them, too. I changed my mind about charity. But I couldn't see a clear path forward in the immediate circumstances, and the urgent needs of the children in our care took all our time, energy, and attention.

Then one day, the ground shook in Haiti. And there, in the destruction and rubble, was the way forward. This was the quiet beginning of something new, something that would eventually become Trades of Hope.

PART ONE

···

HAITI

2002-2010

If you can't feed a hundred people,
then feed just one.

MOTHER TERESA

Chapter One

SHAKEN AND STIRRED

Hold Your Ground

WE HAD FRIENDS OVER FOR DINNER on the evening of January 12, 2010. I still remember sitting around our large square table, laughing at stories from the kids and talking about the latest food plan we were trying, the Daniel Plan. Little did I know my friend Shannon, who was helping me with the work at Three Angels orphanage, kept trying to call my cell phone. She called over and over, but my phone was on silent in another room while we were finishing dinner.

Finally, Shannon called our landline. Surprised by the ring, I answered hesitantly, "Hello?"

"Gretchen, you need to turn on your TV right now and watch the news. There's been an earthquake in Haiti." I could hear the panic in her voice.

I thanked her for calling and told her I would check the news and be in touch later that evening after our guests left.

I tend to stay calm and collected under pressure, a survival skill that helped me navigate challenging situations in more than just this instance. I hung up with Shannon, excused myself from the conversation with our guests, and turned on the TV. There, blaring on every major network channel, was the devastating news of the earthquake in Haiti. It was worse than I could have ever imagined.

At 4:53 pm Eastern Standard Time, an earthquake hit 15 miles south of Port-au-Prince, Haiti, with a magnitude of 7.0 on the Richter scale. Shortly after the initial shock, there were two smaller aftershocks measuring 5.9 and 5.5. Haiti had not experienced an earthquake of this magnitude since 1984, and the results were devastating.

Geologists would later report that the earthquake was the result of a slippage of rock in a small hidden fault under the town of Léogâne, Haiti. Because the initial tremor occurred at a shallow 8.1 miles under the ocean surface, there was an increased shaking effect on the land. The shocks were felt in Haiti and the Dominican Republic, as well as parts of Cuba, Jamaica, and Puerto Rico. Due to their proximity to the initial tremor, Port-au-Prince and other densely populated towns along the Gulf of Gonâve were the most heavily affected. The town of Léogâne, located just west of Port-au-Prince, was essentially leveled.[1] Several small aftershocks continued for weeks, adding to the already hopeless situation.

Now glued to the television and the devastating images online, our friends stayed to watch the news with us, then quietly excused themselves to go home.

I knew our team on the ground at Three Angels would do their very best to deal with the situation. Our house managers had left just days before to come back to the US for a well-deserved month-long respite. The good news was that they had completely stocked the pantry and supplies at the orphanage before leaving, and there was enough food and water to last for weeks. They had even checked the generator recently to make sure it was running well, and there was a good supply of fuel, too. I had no doubt the staff were doing whatever necessary to care for the children . . . if they were all still alive.

Panic set in around 9 pm. I tried calling the orphanage several times but couldn't get through. My mind raced with all of the "what ifs." *What if our buildings collapsed? What if people were trapped? What if the children didn't make it out alive?* At that point—separated by 700-plus miles, a long stretch of ocean, and a two-hour flight—there was nothing I could do except pray.

I spent the evening on the phone and messaging online with adoptive parents, assuring them we were doing everything in our power to make sure the kids were okay. Then I contacted a friend in Haiti, Megan, via Facebook Messenger and asked if she could check on everyone at Three Angels. Megan worked with Three Angels in the past and was now working with a new organization about 45 minutes away from the orphanage. She responded and said she didn't know how but would try to check on the children and staff as soon as she could figure out a way to get there. Cell phone service was down or jammed due to the frenzy of people trying to reach each other, so I didn't know when (or if) I would hear from Megan again, but I was so grateful for her kind response.

Thankfully, another friend, Troy, agreed to give Megan a ride on his motorbike. Megan jumped on the back, and they weaved in and around the rubble in total darkness to get to Three Angels. At times, they didn't know if they were even going to be able to get there. It took two hours instead of the usual 45 minutes, but at about 2 am, my phone rang. I held my breath when I heard Megan's voice, wondering if anyone was still alive.

Relief flooded through my body as she said all of the children and staff at the Angel House were alive, safe, and unharmed. And then Megan described the horrific scene leading up to the orphanage grounds while we spent a few minutes on the phone.

"Gretchen," she said with a heavy sadness in her voice, "There are people everywhere in the streets, sobbing and searching for loved ones. It's not good."

Our buildings were still standing but had huge cracks with gaps of missing cement. It didn't take an engineering degree to know they were uninhabitable. The nannies had immediately taken the children out of the main house, and everyone was together in the neighboring empty lot, where they stayed until morning. After a few tears of relief (okay, maybe more like sobs), I messaged the adoptive parents to let them know the children were safe. I laid back on my pillow, still feeling heavy with emotion, and fell asleep, knowing the days ahead were going to be hard. Even though the physical aftershocks that night had stopped, I knew more emotional shocks would follow in the morning.

Our family moved from California to Palm Coast, Florida, just a few months earlier in 2009 to be closer to Haiti and so that my husband Frits could more easily fly wherever he needed to go as a global consultant. Now Frits was closer to his family in the Netherlands and could fly to Europe almost as fast as to the West Coast. It seemed like the best decision for all practical purposes in that season of our lives. For years, I traveled back and forth, spending at least one week a month in Haiti (five days every five weeks). As our kids got older, they were able to travel with me on occasion, too. Those are still some of my favorite memories with Elisabeth, Harrison, and Mia.

When I woke up early on Wednesday, January 13, 2010—less than 12 hours after the earthquake hit Haiti—I knew I had one choice: *figure out a way to get there as fast as possible.* I needed to see for myself that the children were okay and make sure the staff had the supplies and resources they needed to keep everyone fed. One of the major news outlets, CNN, was starting to report on the scarcity of supplies, including drinking water. At that point, I didn't even know if the staff could safely retrieve the food we had in the pantry area.

The rising sun and continuing aftershocks revealed just how much damage had been done. Haitian construction crews didn't always use the high standards we are accustomed to in the US. In fact, in the months after the earthquake, experts attributed the mass devastation to an extremely low amount of rebar and poor-quality cement mixture used in block construction throughout the country.[2] Most homes and commercial buildings over one story had collapsed with the tremors, which meant a majority of middle-class Haitian families were homeless. Even working professionals, like our school's headmaster, Alix, now had no place to live.

Due to the extreme poverty and violence in Haiti, most properties in Port-au-Prince were surrounded by seven to ten-foot cement block walls. These walls lined almost every street around the city, and the vendors set up shop against them, selling freshly grilled food, used clothing, or household goods—everything from laundry soap to colanders. When the earthquake happened, the walls toppled over, injuring or killing an unknown number of women, men, and children while they were working their businesses. By all accounts, this was beyond horrific. Thankfully, no one was hurt on our property. While our buildings were still standing, our security walls were not.

When I saw the images on TV, I could not believe that *all* of our kids and staff were unharmed and accounted for—thank goodness and thank God! The children were moved to safety by our incredible team. The staff also managed to pull supplies out of the recently restocked pantry, but they did it quickly, not knowing if the buildings were about to collapse. They found we had enough water, snacks, rice, and oatmeal to go around.

One of our volunteers, Abbey McArthur, was less than a mile away, exercising at another school with her American friends, when the earthquake happened. Fifteen minutes later, amidst the destruction around her, Abbey crawled over rubble to get back to the orphanage. In an interview with TIME Magazine a few weeks after the earthquake, Abbey described her experience as though "It felt like God had picked up the earth and was just shaking it back and forth."[3] Abbey was halfway through her one-year teaching commitment at the Three Angels School. When she finally got to Angel House, she was so relieved to see the main building still standing. Francois Jean Louis, a translator for the orphanage, told her the kids were all safe and had been relocated to a neighbor's field. Abbey found everyone and was surprised at how calm they were, especially for children ranging in age from 5 months to 9 years. Some babies were still asleep in their nanny's arms. Some little ones were giggling and playing together as if nothing had happened. The adults knew the devastating realities of what had just happened and were really scared. Abby was both thankful and amazed no one had been injured in the quake.

Like most of the city, the children and staff would spend the night outside in the neighbor's field. The next day, they got permission to move to the protection of nearby Quisqueya Christian School for five nights, sleeping with blankets and pillows on a concrete floor under a tin roof on the porch. The school's security walls were still standing, and with all of the uncertainty in the streets, we wanted (and needed) the safety those walls would provide.

That morning after the sun rose, Abbey called from Quisqueya to tell me the news I half-expected to hear.

"The kids are still safe; no one was even hurt. But there are huge cracks in the walls, and it's not safe to go back inside the orphanage."

Later, when I went to see the buildings myself, I saw cracks so deep that paper notes could have been passed through the walls. I still couldn't believe everyone made it out unharmed and alive with everything that fell to the ground during the earthquake. Eventually, like almost every multi-story structure still standing in Port-au-Prince, our building would be condemned. Engineers would soon confirm that Angel House had to be demolished. It was the Japanese UN who eventually brought in excavation equipment to tear it down. But at the moment, our greatest concern was care for the kids.

I knew I had to find a way into Haiti soon, but all the airlines had immediately and indefinitely canceled flights in and out of Port-au-Prince. So I made a few phone calls. First, I called Harold, a guy I knew who ran a small airline company called Mission Flights International. MFI was a Florida-based organization that had been supporting missionary efforts in the Caribbean since 1964, predominantly in Haiti and the Dominican Republic. They mostly flew cargo planes carrying medical and humanitarian supplies into hard-to-reach places. But NASCAR team owner Rick Hendrick, who knew Harold, offered the use of his own two turboprop aircraft, able to accommodate 45 passengers each, along with ten pilots and their crew members who all volunteered to fly back and forth to Haiti. According to TIME, Hendrick had thrown his planes into disaster relief before, including over a thousand hours of support after Hurricane Katrina.[4] Harold worked to increase his passenger flight capacity through other pilots and organizations, too. He returned my call to say he thought he could get us a few seats on one of these planes by Saturday, January 16. I packed a quick bag and showed up at dawn at the Fort Pierce Airport that Saturday morning.

I met Mitch, Kevin, and Rob at the airport. Mitch[5] was the house manager and lived at the orphanage with his wife Monica[6] but had been back in the US for a few days. He was also a doctor. Rob was a registered nurse from Michigan, and Kevin was a pastor and adoptive dad who lived in New Smyrna, Florida. Kevin and his wife were in the process of adopting two children at Three Angels. All three men willingly agreed to travel with me to check on the children and staff. Elisabeth, who was 15 at the time, begged to go with me and help. Her eyes filled with tears when I thanked her but told her no.

"Honey," I said, "the planes that can land in Haiti right now need to be filled with doctors, nurses, and construction workers because they're the only people who can do what's needed to help. We need to take up as few seats as possible."

This broke her heart, but she understood. Honestly, I also had no idea what it would be like in Haiti. I didn't want to subject her to something traumatic or incredibly dangerous. But I was so proud of her for wanting to jump into action and make sure the kids were okay. I understood because I was anxious to get to Haiti, too.

The airport in Fort Pierce was packed with Haitians trying to get home and humanitarian relief workers trying to bring aid and medical supplies. With tears running down his cheeks, one Haitian man told me that his wife, three daughters, and mother were all at Mass when the large cement church they were in fell to the ground. He was trying to get home to bury the five women he loved the most. I sat next to him in silence, absorbing some of his sorrow, as busy World Vision staffers and medical professionals moved around us, talking loudly on cell phones with their contacts in Haiti. There was so much sadness in that little airport and a lot of nervous energy.

The earthquake knocked out runway lights in Port-au-Prince, and debris littered all of the runways except one. This meant that flights were limited to daylight hours. Close to sunset, we knew our chance to get into Haiti that day had passed. Rob, Mitch, and I booked a couple of rooms at the Hampton Inn and went to the local Cracker Barrel for dinner. That night, Mitch prayed words I'll never forget because they hit a tender spot of disbelief and perhaps more than a little cynicism deep inside me. With his head bowed and hands folded on the table, Mitch prayed,

"Lord, please help us to bring all of the children home!"

My immediate thought was, *Oh my God, Mitch. What are you even talking about?! Like that's ever going to happen!* I had too many run-ins with the Haitian government and the US Embassy to know it was nearly impossible to believe for even one second that our kids could travel back to the US with us. But I nodded along during the prayer. We sat quietly, eating our chicken pot pies and turkey dinners.

Harold called me during dinner to say he believed he had a spot for us on a flight leaving early the next morning, but we had to be there before sunrise so they could get as many flights in as possible that day. That was the news we were hoping to hear!

We met Harold at the airport just before dawn on Sunday, January 17. It was obvious Harold hadn't slept much in previous days, but he greeted us with a smile and a few encouraging words as we waited to board one of the small turboprop flights. Our morning departure turned into an afternoon takeoff, including a fuel stop on another Caribbean island on the way to Haiti. Refueling was necessary just in case we spent a long time circling in the sky, waiting for our turn to land. Due to all of the flights attempting to get in and out of Haiti, we were lucky we made it out that day. With more air traffic to manage than usual, only one runway cleared, and limited daylight hours, our window to land in Haiti was coming to a close. I was concerned we would run out of time and be forced to turn around.

As it turned out, we landed in plenty of time with enough fleeting daylight to see the destruction the earthquake left in its wake.

ON THE GROUND IN HAITI

The airport in Port-au-Prince was still standing, but the runways were a mess with piles of concrete and rubble spread out as far as I could see. We made our way through the small airport, and when we stepped onto the street, *no one* was there. Port-au-Prince was like a ghost town, which felt eerie compared to the typical hustle and bustle. I didn't know how we were even getting from the airport to the school grounds where our kids and staff were staying. Megan and I had been texting about our arrival time when we stopped for gas in the Caribbean, but I had no idea if she had received the message. I was so relieved to see her standing just outside the airport gates. Megan even found a driver with a little red rusty pickup truck, called a tap-tap to transport our supplies. I was so grateful.

After hugging her tightly, we took the 30-minute ride to the school. From the back of the pick up truck, I couldn't get over the destruction I saw all around us. Cement block walls that once lined the streets were now in pieces all over the roads creating an obstacle course. Small stretches of road had already been cleared, but getting around the rubble was still very hard. Gas station overhangs had collapsed, crushing everything below them. You could still see pieces of the cars sticking out from underneath. It made me wonder where their owners were and what happened to them. The hopeless look of Haitians wandering the streets brought tears to our eyes. People were in shock from all they had lost as they searched for loved ones who had now been missing for almost five days.

So much was just *gone*.

The Three Angels staff and children were still safely inside the gates of Quisqueya Christian School down the street from the orphanage. There was a set of classrooms with a bathroom and a large cement porch with an overhang. And this is where all 26 kids and their nannies stayed in the days following the earthquake. By the time I arrived, now five days later, the kids were having a great time playing on the outdoor playground. They loved the dome-shaped climbing structure and the slides. I think they thought it was a fun field trip with an extended sleepover. Little did they know their lives would never be the same again.

When we realized everything was going well—the kids were being cared for, well-fed, and genuinely having a great time—Mitch and Rob started treating a few people around the property who were wounded. I remember seeing a man come through the gates with his arm moving like jello. I thought, *Dear God, this man has been living like this for five days! How could he still be upright and walking around?* I could have passed out just looking at him! A few blocks away, our medical clinic still stood intact on the grounds of Three Angels. It had been built like a fortress, so it wasn't surprising that it was still standing in solid condition. Mitch and Rob took the man to the clinic with casting supplies and, thankfully, reset his arm. They casted a few other people and cleaned and bandaged some open wounds. It didn't cover the multitude of injuries since the earthquake, but it helped.

While Mitch and Rob were at the clinic and Kevin was playing with the kids, I took turns holding the little ones while talking with the staff. One of the nannies came through the gate looking sad. Another staff member told us the woman's son had just died. I set the toddler I was holding on the ground and walked over to the nanny with one of the guys who worked with me so he could translate. My Creole was still limited to about a 2-year-old's speaking capabilities. Through heavy tears, she told me about her nine-year-old son, who was hit in the head with a piece of cement during the earthquake. He seemed fine after it happened. But a day later, he died unexpectedly. We held each other and cried for what seemed like forever, standing in the middle of the playground with the children singing and running around us. In my limited Creole, I told her I was so sorry. It felt a bit ridiculous to say, but there really were no good words. I didn't know her son, and I barely knew her. She hadn't been with Three Angels very long, but I asked if she wanted us to pray together. She said yes, so we prayed through our sobs in English and a bit of Creole. We hugged again, and then she went off to talk with her colleagues and friends.

After a few days at the school, we were getting pressure from Quisqueya to find another place to house the children and staff. Doctors Without Borders was setting up a mobile hospital on the school's huge soccer fields the next day, and we could no longer stay on the grounds. I was told it was against Doctors Without Borders' policies to have additional people in an area where they would be treating patients. I went to bed wondering what we were going to do. God was going to have to provide an answer because I had none.

That night, Sunday, January 17, just as I was drifting off to sleep, one of the young American teachers serving at Three Angels came to wake me up. It was a call from my friend Shannon in the US, who had been working to contact the embassy on our behalf.

"Gretchen," she said, "I just received word from the US Embassy. If you're there by 8 am with all of the kids and their documentation, the embassy will grant everyone humanitarian parole."

The possibility was so big and crazy that I immediately knew *this was our one and only shot*. I didn't know of any place left on this island for us to go. I was also very concerned that adoptions would be put on hold indefinitely. If we were ever going to make it out of Haiti with all of the kids at one time, it was going to have to be now. *This was it*. Little did I know just how many hours Shannon and Cara, one of our adoptive moms, spent on the phone to fast-track the visa process. They called every politician and agency they thought could help to beg for our visas. Eventually, they got in contact with the U.S. Citizenship and Immigration Services (USCIS), which operated out of the Department of Homeland Security. Together, they forged a plan involving humanitarian parole.[7] This was a best-case scenario in a worst-case situation.

When the earthquake happened, all 26 children at the orphanage were already in the process of being adopted by families in the United States and Canada. And now the US Embassy was telling us we could bring them all home on humanitarian parole. Humanitarian parole meant that individuals outside the United States could request or be granted parole into the US based on urgent humanitarian reasons.[8] Mitch's prayer was on the verge of coming true, and I still wasn't sure I could believe it.

We needed to go to the orphanage and pick up all of the children's collection of adoption paperwork (called *dossiers*), but first, we needed to secure transportation for all 30 of us in the morning.

I begged the school official in charge of transportation at Quisqueya to help us. The school had one large truck-type vehicle, and they were hesitant to loan it to us. I understood. Not only was it their only truck, but they also needed it first thing in the morning. So, I offered a sizable donation to the school to show our appreciation and agreed to go a couple of hours earlier than necessary to make sure the vehicle was returned by the time they needed it. We were all shaken in the days following the earthquake, but I knew I had to hold my ground with this request if we wanted to get the children to safety. I made the offer, assuring him of the early departure, and stood quietly for what seemed like forever. I'm sure I had a sad, pathetic look on my face, waiting for the school official's reply. He finally agreed. Thank God.

Gathering all of the documentation required by the US Embassy was the next hurdle; one we had to jump in the dark of night. Thankfully, Mitch and Monica[9] had recently organized all the paperwork and documentation for every single child. The three of us walked to the orphanage in the early morning hours, using flashlights to pull files and put them into large plastic containers. It probably wasn't the safest thing I've ever done, but we had to do it if we wanted to be at the embassy before 8 am on Monday, January 19. It took a few hours of working in the dark, but sunrise was getting closer. Finally, we had everything we needed and were ready to load the kids up and get them to the US Embassy, located just down the road from the airport.

With our bins full of documentation, we returned to Quisqueya to wake the children and say goodbye to their nannies. This was really emotional. These women had been the stand-in moms for these little ones, for *years* in some cases. And all of a sudden, we were scooping them up and whisking them away to the airport. Nothing about the journey was easy for anyone involved. Tears were shed all around. After a bumpy ride in the back of the huge truck with metal caging on the sides, we were sitting outside the embassy doors by 6 am.

Waiting anywhere for a long time with 26 children, ages five months to nine years old, was a lot to ask, let alone in the middle of the worst kind of chaos. I was friendly to every UN staff member who passed us as they went through the gates into the embassy. Lots of smiling, more "Good Mornings!" than I could count, and a huge dose of eye contact. I wasn't sure who was going to help us that day, but I did know I didn't want to be forgotten on the curb.

At about 9 am, an embassy employee ushered us into the waiting area. Rob, Kevin, and the older kids moved the chairs to create a makeshift play area. In reality, they were just trying to keep everyone contained and corralled. The embassy even provided MREs (meals ready to eat) and bottles of water for everyone. We started feeding the little ones when I heard someone call my name. A staff member showed us into a small room. I asked Mitch to come with me as he had been working on all of the adoption paperwork for months. On the other side of the plexiglass window, an employee started going through every single piece of paper in each and every file. This process took hours to ensure each child had adequate documentation and was legally allowed to leave the country. Finally, the gentleman helping us looked up and said he had everything he needed. *What? They weren't going to give us a list of items we were missing and make this impossible?* He said he and his staff would begin processing the visas. Mitch and I walked out of the little room to the waiting area with the rambunctious kids. I felt numb with disbelief. *Was this actually happening?*

A few more hours passed, and I was called up to the window again. The embassy agent told me we'd get all of the visas in hand when I had confirmation of an airplane willing and available to fly us out of the country that day. Well, that was great, but Shannon and I had been talking throughout the afternoon, and no private pilot would commit to coming to get us unless we had the visas in hand. It was a humanitarian crisis catch-22. I thought I was going to cry. *Was this really going to be the reason we couldn't get the kids out?* At that moment, it seemed like it. But we weren't giving up. We had families across the country searching for an answer on our behalf. In the end, Harold had the solution.

The Hendrick Motorsports flight team was still taking rescue mission flights back and forth between Florida and Haiti. They heard from Harold that we were desperate for a ride and had 26 Haitian children. They agreed to guarantee our flight back to the US but said the offer was only good for the next 60 minutes because they had to take off before dusk. They would only wait for us if we had the visas in hand. Shannon called me while I was standing in the embassy office to tell me the great news. I turned back to the US Embassy officer to tell him we had a confirmed ride, while Shannon called the Hendrick Motorsports team and told them we had all of the visas. Okay, we didn't *actually* have the visas in hand yet, but I could see them on the other side of the plexiglass window. The embassy agent handed me all 26 visas and ushered us onto their fancy coach bus, complete with air-conditioning and red velvet curtains. This bus usually transported dignitaries and world officials, but that day it transported us.

The whole thing was surreal, and the kids thought it was an amazing adventure! There were giggles of excitement as we drove onto the tarmac and walked up the stairs, with a child on our hip or holding hands, onto the private plane. I remember double-checking that everyone was safe and secure in a seat, then buckled my own seat while holding one of the smaller babies in my lap. I let out a sigh of exhaustion and relief. Mitch and I had been awake for about 36 hours at that point. One little girl, Bethany, started crying, terrified of being strapped into her seat with the noise of the plane beginning to roar. One of the Hendrick flight attendants sat in front of Bethany on the floor to comfort her. I'm sure this was against flight protocol, but I was so touched by her compassion. We got everyone buckled in, and the pilot took off just before the flight crew didn't have enough daylight. It was a potentially dangerous situation for the pilots and their flight crews to get stuck on the dark runway in Port-au-Prince. I'm forever grateful the crew waited *just for us*. This kind act changed the lives of 26 children and their new families.

I still remember looking out the window at the sky, a beautiful bright fiery orange from the setting sun. My eyes were full of tears. As they fell, I forced a smile on my face to reassure the frightened baby girl in my lap that everything was going to be alright as she turned her head to look up at me.

Shaken and stirred, we stood our ground in those moments of uncertainty before boarding that plane. I knew it was what I needed to do, what *we* needed to do, to get those kids home. Staying in Haiti under rubble and in chaos was no longer an option. My prayer in those moments was that these kids would one day understand, perhaps when they were all grown, why we had to leave so quickly. Hopefully, one day, when they hear the stories and see pictures of the damage, they will know we made the best decisions we could with their safety, care, and well-being in mind—to lift them out of a place that could no longer be their home.

ON THE GROUND IN THE US

We landed in Florida three hours later. It was probably around 7:30-8 pm EST. The adoptive families had been frantically scrambling all day to get to the little Fort Pierce airport in hopes we could secure visas for the children. They caught last-minute flights from all over the country, flying into larger airports like Orlando and then driving to Fort Pierce. Most of them were already at Fort Pierce watching as we walked down the airplane stairs, across the tarmac, and into the airport. The night sky was dark, but that didn't stop friends and family from lining up alongside the adoptive families to greet us and welcome their kids home. I couldn't believe so many of my local friends were there, just on the other side of the fence.

I was so exhausted and relieved that I hadn't even thought about what would happen once we landed. My primary focus had been landing on US soil. But this was a better homecoming than I could ever have imagined. We got everyone off the plane and thanked the team from Hendrick Motorsports over and over again. They didn't have to go to Haiti, let alone wait for us on that hot tarmac in Port-au-Prince. One by one, ICE Agents checked IDs and visas for all of the children to make sure the proper families were picking up the appropriate child. Then, everyone left to go home. There were tears all around, so many tears. Tears of relief, overwhelm, exhaustion, and gratitude.

Just like Mitch prayed, we were able to bring every single child home to the US from Port-au-Prince just days after the earthquake, thanks to the humanitarian parole visas issued by the US government.

The adoptive families finished the adoption process with their children living in their homes. We followed up with these families in the coming days and weeks with care and encouragement, in person and over the phone. The silver lining of this situation was that these kids were no longer stuck in the Haitian system, where it typically took three to four years to process adoptions. Every child was able to go home and start their life with their forever family.

All of a sudden, I didn't have an orphanage anymore.

....

Chapter Two

WISE INSTINCTS

Trust Your Gut

YEARS BEFORE THE EARTHQUAKE, I fell in love with the idea of microfinancing. I just wasn't sure how to make it all work with what we were doing at Three Angels. When all of the children in our care were placed with their adoptive families literally overnight, just a few days after the earthquake, I had a decision to make. *I could rebuild and keep doing what we were doing. Or I could pivot and do something else (and all of the* Friends *fans said: Pivot!).* I had a strong sense of what to do next, but it meant trusting my instincts.

Microfinancing wasn't a thought that came to me out of thin air. During our days running the orphanage in Haiti, I read a book by Muhammed Yunus called *Banker to the Poor.* Yunus told real stories of real women who built businesses and provided for themselves and their families thanks to the help of small business loans. As a result, most, if not all, of these women alleviated the poverty they were experiencing with their own businesses. That's when it hit me. *If we don't want women giving up their children as poverty orphans, we need to create opportunities for women to provide for their families and live better lives.* This is something many of us take for granted in the US. Compared to many other countries, we have significantly more job opportunities to pursue a good life. I wanted to help women outside the US have jobs so they could keep their children, raise those children, and get out of difficult and often dangerous situations.

We ended up creating an online marketplace to sell handmade fashion and home accessories instead of microfinancing, but that's where the idea started. That light-bulb moment after reading *Banker to the Poor* eventually turned into a new business model with fair-trade fashion and Artisan Partners around the world. And where was our first official partnership formed? Yep, you guessed it. *Haiti.*

But my ideas to make the world a better place, particularly for women and children in developing countries, didn't start in Haiti. Those ideas began in the small town of Midland, Michigan, in the smack-dab middle of America.

I grew up the oldest of two kids, with a brother named Michael, who is four years younger than me. At times I acted like a bossy big sister, and other times, like his second mom. *I'm sure he loved that!* I was the daughter of a working mother and father who both shared in our loving and secure care. Michael and I spent summers traipsing around the woods between our house and our grandparents' house across the pond. We were a typical family from the Midwest and of British-German descent, like nearly everyone around us. While growing up, our home life felt typical and boring. I've since learned that, unfortunately, *boring* and *typical* were unusual. As an adult, I now know that many people in our world grow up experiencing chaotic, abusive homes. I've learned to appreciate my upbringing in a safe, loving environment. I think it gave me a sense of strength and confidence that others sometimes struggle to find.

I thought I could be anything I wanted to be when I grew up. In fact, I still remember dancing in front of the large mirror in our living room as a young teen, thinking I wanted to do three things in my life:

earn a spot as captain of the pom-pom squad in high school, apply for a coveted internship at nearby Dow Chemical Company, and adopt children from far away—perhaps after a stint in the Peace Corps.

A church missions trip to Jamaica during my senior year with a nearby youth group only confirmed the last one. *Why would anyone choose to give birth when there were babies all over the world who needed a family?!* I still remember the feeling I had as a kid watching all of those Save the Children commercials about starving children in Africa, thinking what I wouldn't do to give my squash to them for two reasons: first, to clear my dinner plate, (I really didn't like the acorn squash my Grandpa filled my mom's car with every year) and second, to help their swollen bellies with food from my Grandpa's garden.

By the time high school graduation rolled around, my parents had split up. Not because of their disagreements but more because of their indifference toward one another. At least, that's the way it seemed to me. The day my mom filed for divorce wasn't a shock to my sixteen-year-old self, but for Michael, who was twelve at the time, it seemed like a bigger deal. Even after the divorce, I still thought of us as a loving, secure family. Michael and I lived with my mom, but it was Michael who did most of the weekend and evening visits to my dad's house. I guess I thought I had other things to do with my busy teenage life. My dad and I eventually drifted apart, and I haven't had much contact with him since. It is what it is, and I'm okay with that. I loved my parents dearly from day one, and I'm so grateful for the way they raised us. After the divorce, Mom kept working for the telephone company Michigan Bell in different administrative positions. But her love life moved on, and she eventually got married to Earl, who brought three daughters with him. This meant I went from being the oldest to somewhere in the middle. And by the way, they aren't wicked stepsisters at all. Jen, Sara, and Kristen have become my family. They are my *sisters*.

Faith has always played a crucial role in my upbringing. We belonged to a local Catholic parish in town, that is, until my parents got a divorce, and my mom found out she was required to pay for an annulment if she wanted to keep taking communion. This didn't sit well with her after serving, tithing, and attending for so many years. And I can understand why. I loved that little church. It was my spiritual home and where I truly found my faith. But I also felt drawn in awkward and emotional ways to the charismatic youth group in the next town over. I took my first mission trip to Jamaica with this group, which was definitely a formative experience.

Looking back, I realize it was the parish priest at our Catholic church, Father Tom, who taught me about God's love for us and that it's okay to ask questions and think for ourselves. I believe this allowed me to have conversations with God in my everyday life. I didn't need to recite liturgical prayers. I knew God wanted a relationship with me, with or without those rote prayers. The discussions we had with Father Tom in Catechism class would shape the rest of my life in small and profound ways. He was probably considered "progressive," even by today's standards, because he cared more about teaching us how to love people like Jesus than giving us a list of what we were supposed to be against as Christians. Perhaps this is why, at twenty years of age, I felt a little bit nervous but nowhere near shame when I had to tell my grandmother I was pregnant and not married.

The summer before my senior year of high school, I earned that internship at Dow Chemical. Dow's international headquarters were in Midland, Michigan. Growing up, it seemed everyone worked for Dow or companies with big contracts at Dow. My plan after high school was to keep working at Dow, go to Delta Community College, then on to Central Michigan University. I had no idea what I wanted to major in, but I knew I was going to college. It never occurred to me that I would later make a choice that inadvertently derailed that decision. I was seventeen the summer I started my Dow internship. I didn't realize it at the time, but I ended up on a prestigious, global project, which was a *big deal*. I got to know many successful executives from all over the world. I also got to know some of the international contractors.

Frits Huijskens was one of the Dutch SAP consultants. I started seeing an interesting European guy around the building. He seemed quiet and moody. Later, I learned that he had just lost his mom, and after spending a few months back in the Netherlands, he was still a bit heavy with grief. It kind of added to the mystique, though. *You can see where this is going, can't you?* One Friday afternoon, Frits met a friend at the office. They were going to a Detroit Pistons basketball game that night. As he was heading out the door, Frits introduced me to his friend and jokingly said, "I'm going to marry that girl one day." *Um, what?! I barely knew this guy!* He said it with a smirking grin just to rattle me, and boy, did it work! I was embarrassed, horrified…and, to be honest, a bit giddy.

Over time, the kind and adventurous side of Frits came out. He talked a lot about skiing. So, we decided to hit the slopes together one weekend. As the saying goes, it was all downhill from there. But, you know, in a good way!

We had a great time riding up the chair lift and skiing down the side of Crystal Mountain over and over again. (It's Michigan—the hills are only so big.) As dusk was closing in, we put our skis, boots, and extra gear in Frits' Ford Probe (yep, he was cool with that Ford Probe). A big "Sale" sign was glowing from the window of the ski shop, and Frits mentioned he would like to check for new ski pants.

You don't need to ask me twice to go shopping. We stuffed our wet ski gear into the trunk of the Probe and went into the shop. A little while later, we walked back to the car empty-handed. Frits checked his pockets for the keys. They weren't there. We searched the shop and outside the car, only to realize his keys were gone. We knew we had those keys when we put our gear in the car. And now the car was locked with our things inside. Frits then remembered setting the keys on top of the car and realized he must have left them there. After checking the lost and found at the front desk and looking around some more, Frits casually said, "They're gone. Okay, where can we find a rental car? We can drive back home tonight, and I can come up with the second set tomorrow and pick up my car." I thought, *Wait, what?? You mean you can have inconveniences like this happen and not get really mad?* While all of the men in my family were good men and would never physically hurt anyone, they had tempers that flared in moments like this. And once they got mad, they stayed mad, acting grouchy for a long time. But Frits didn't do this. His mood didn't swing, and he didn't get angry. He decided how he would take care of it in a calm, logical way. I'm pretty sure I fell a tiny bit in love with him that night.

After that weekend of skiing, Frits and I spent more and more time together. At some point, I knew I was falling hard for him and suspected he was falling for me, too. We started spending every evening and weekend together. After this had been going on for weeks, I realized that we had never even turned on a television. I don't know how we possibly found so many things to talk about, but we talked for hours on end, day after day. We skied, ate way too much pizza (oh, to be young and able to eat as much pizza as you want), and told each other everything about ourselves. Frits quickly became my best friend, despite our age difference.

I gave up my internship when I transferred to Central Michigan University. It was too much of a drive, and the snowy commute made my mom nervous. So I started working in a nearby art gallery, attending full-time school, and still seeing Frits. We spent every spare moment together, between his full-time job and my part-time gig, and status as a full-time student. After about two years of dating, Frits decided he wanted to spend time with his aging father in the Netherlands. So, he talked Dow Chemical into allowing him to work on the same project from Belgium in an office about an hour away from the village he grew up in. I went to visit him for most of the summer just before my junior year of college. We spent our days exploring the area and soaking up time together, traveling all over Amsterdam, Paris, and Antwerp, Belgium.

One of the most romantic evenings we spent was in Antwerp. We had dinner in a tiny, old stone restaurant next to Our Lady Cathedral in the center of town. The restaurant was called Het Vermoeide Model (The Tired Model), based on an oil painting of a monk painting a valiant portrait of a cardinal while he dozed off in his chair. It's hard to say when the restaurant building was constructed, but the cathedral's construction started in the 1300s and wasn't finished until 1521. There are few things that wooed this Michigan girl more than beautiful, antiquated architecture. The restaurant's interior was decorated with sparkling chandeliers, candlelight, and music from the black baby grand in the middle of the room. Everything was perfect. Over a bottle of red wine, Frits and I began talking about our plans for the future. I was determined to finish my degree at CMU. Frits wanted to spend another year or so in the Netherlands, and then we decided we'd get married and move to California. We wanted to be able to explore the West Coast more. We'd been together for two and a half years at this point, and everything seemed to be working out well. We had a plan.

Just a few weeks later, I would be so happy we had that conversation in the romantic little restaurant in Antwerp.

I flew home to Michigan that August, just in time to start the fall semester. I was miserable because I thought I wouldn't see Frits until Thanksgiving break. We were going to meet for a week in Bonaire, an island 50 miles off the coast of Venezuela. At that time, Bonaire was part of the Netherlands. We had been there once before together, exploring the arid landscapes, snorkeling, and reading books on the beach. Not a bad way to spend the week. I was very much looking forward to it. But at that point, our time in Bonaire seemed incredibly far away.

The flight back to Midland, Michigan, would have been much more enjoyable if I had known I would see Frits again in about a week. Just a few days later, as I was buying my college books and moving into my dorm room, I was not feeling well. I thought it was a sinus infection, but during a brief check-up at the doctor's office on campus, my world changed in an instant.

I was *pregnant*.

I told my mom about the news right away, even before calling Frits. We didn't have cell phones then, and thankfully my mom was in her office just down the street.

Suddenly, my plan—*our plan*—was turned upside down. Remember, *I wanted to adopt babies, not give birth to them!* I don't know if I ever said that out loud, but it was always the thought on my mind when it came to raising babies. I was going to finish my degree and then get married. And *then* start to think about children. *That was the plan.*

A twinge of panic set in. Not only was I pregnant, but the doctor said that, based on the heartbeat, I was already sixteen weeks along! (Yes, as a grown woman, I now realize it was ridiculous to be pregnant for sixteen weeks and not realize it). I can tell you that I was 100% in shock by this new reality. As I drove to my mom's office, I bawled nearly the entire way. *I had a plan, and a baby was not yet a part of it.* As soon as I stepped into the office, my mom saw me walk in, looked at me, and immediately asked me to join her in a private office. She knew I had been at the doctor that morning and could tell something was wrong. I will always admire her for how she responded. First, she had a flash of anger on her face; then, I saw a flash of sadness. What followed was a look of compassionate determination as she fixed her eyes on mine and said,

"Okay, Gretchen, what are you going to do?"

I drove home to the house my mom shared with my step dad and called Frits. This news was quite a surprise just a few days before his 30th birthday. The very next morning, Frits was on the first flight from Amsterdam to Michigan to be with me. This was clearly *not* the plan. Then I did the hardest thing—I told my great-grandma the big news. Granted, My mom told me I had to, or I probably would have just waited until the baby showed up. I wasn't nervous because I was afraid of her. I was nervous because she was the sweetest person I had ever known, and I hated the idea of disappointing her. As I shared my news through tears, I saw the concern in her eyes, but she hugged me hard and told me she knew I would be a great mother. That's when I went back to the doctor's office to confirm the details via ultrasound with Frits. Yep, I was really sixteen weeks pregnant.

When Frits arrived, he hugged me hard and assured me everything would be okay. We would figure this out together. So what if things were happening out of order? We spent every waking moment together over the next few days talking through our plans and preparing for the baby we would later call our "best surprise ever." After hours of talking, I realized Frits wasn't ready to leave his aging father in the Netherlands. This meant one thing: if we wanted to be together, the right thing for me to do was move there.

I stayed in Michigan for some necessary follow-up doctor's appointments, and Frits flew back across the Atlantic to work. The baby had a ventricle in her brain (yes, we were having a baby *girl*) that was slightly enlarged compared to average sizes. It turned out to be nothing, but I still needed some advanced imaging and follow-up visits. In hindsight, it worked out okay to have a few weeks in the US to catch my breath and get used to the idea, even to be happy about the idea, of having a baby before making a huge move to the Netherlands.

At twenty weeks pregnant, I moved to the quaint Dutch village of Lewedorp to be with Frits in his tiny house and his family in neighboring houses. And I quickly found myself living in the "fishbowl" of a tiny community. Frits' mother and father had moved to Lewedorp from an eastern province thirty years earlier to take over a milk delivery and grocery business. They were entrepreneurs who raised three boys and taught them to be good men with great work ethics. Frits was the youngest.

Five days a week, Frits commuted to his office in Antwerp, Belgium. For me, this meant long days of wandering around the village under the watchful eye of every observant woman nearby. Needless to say, the village lost its quaintness quickly. Few people were comfortable speaking English, and I didn't speak much Dutch. And I swear, everywhere I went, people just stood and stared at me, especially older women who would peek from behind curtains when I walked by on my way to the bakery. It seemed as though everyone was peering out their windows, saying, *There goes that pregnant American girl again!* I realize some of this was my own insecurity, but I am telling you, those ladies were *not* subtle. Eventually, I started driving a few kilometers away to a bigger town just to catch my breath, buy a few groceries, and blend in without everyone staring at me.

When it came time to have my baby girl, I had the craziest little female doctor in the village *at my bedside*. Literally, at my bedside. She made house calls. With her short, spiky hair and big round glasses, she was caring but abrupt and rough. To add to the oddity of giving birth in a foreign hospital, pain medications were not an option in rural Dutch communities at the time. Thankfully, what started with my water breaking at about 1 pm ended with a beautiful baby girl by 7 pm. She was three weeks early but alert and sweet, with a head full of dark hair and square cheeks. Within minutes after I gave birth to our baby, the doctor jumped up on the table, straddled over me, and aggressively massaged my abdomen until the afterbirth was released into the bedpan at the end of the table. Somehow, I knew if she had just given it a minute, it would have been released without her painful intervention, but she didn't ask my opinion. It was quite the whirlwind experience!

Frits and I named our baby girl Elisabeth. I still wasn't sure how I wanted to spell it. Elizabeth is typical in America, but Elisabeth is common in Europe. So, she doesn't know it, but a random nurse ultimately decided (*surprise, Elisabeth!*). Here's how it happened: the next day, when they brought Elisabeth to my room after a morning exam, she had a little hand-written bracelet with "Elisabeth Huijskens" on it. I took that as a sign. It was promptly decided that she would be Elisabeth, *not* Elizabeth. My mom still tells the story of how she needed to have the Z in Elizabeth plucked out and replaced with an S on the monogrammed, satin-trimmed blanket she had ordered. Oops!

The nurses helped me change Elisabeth and gave me tips on how to take care of her. This was so helpful because I hadn't been around many babies up to that point. I still remember the first diaper change. I was so awkward and slow with her diaper that suddenly, there was a huge mess everywhere. (*TMI, Elisabeth?*) The nurse and I were laughing so hard we were crying. Cleaning things up the best I could, I then realized the nurse was filling the sink with water intending to give Elisabeth a bath. This was a moment where I wished so badly I knew how to speak Dutch fluently. I remembered reading that you shouldn't fully bathe a baby until the umbilical cord had fallen off. It was somewhere in one of the dozens of books I bought when I first found out I was pregnant. I didn't even know why bathing was a bad thing. I just remember not being able to get my words out fast enough to ask her to stop. I watched as she bathed Elisabeth and just kept thinking, *"Well, they are the professionals. Not me."* But sure enough, Elisabeth got an infection in her umbilical cord. A day or so after we were released, we brought her back to the hospital with a high fever, and they took her straight to the NICU. Thank goodness for the Dutch nanny provided by the hospital who came to check on us every day. She noticed Elisabeth's weakness as a sign of infection and the need for immediate care. I just thought Elisabeth was a really sleepy baby. After some testing, we found out she had a staph infection.

I remember talking to my mom and stepdad on the phone during those days while Elisabeth was still in the hospital. Frits and I would call my parents every evening with updates. I thought it was weird that my stepdad Earl asked, *"How are you doing?"* the way he did. So serious. I told him we were doing well and Elisabeth was getting antibiotics and would soon be fine. I didn't realize how dire the situation had become and how serious staph infections could be until years later. At the time, I thought her infection was the equivalent of an ear infection. (I know, I know. In my defense, I was very young, and Google wasn't a thing yet). Elisabeth recovered well, but I'm still thankful for the hospital nanny who showed up to check on us in the days following her birth. The home-visit service I didn't even think I needed turned out to be a huge gift. Looking back, I wish I had trusted my instincts and spoke up, but without knowing Dutch, I'm not sure what good it would have done.

We lived in Lewedorp for almost a year before moving to Westchester County, New York. We lived there for two years, then in Malaysia for six months, before returning to the Netherlands again. That's the beauty of Frits' work. We could live almost anywhere at any time. I still remember the sights, smells, and sounds of the big high-rise in Malaysia. Most of our building was filled with people from all over the world. It felt like one big vacation with all of the American, British, and Australian families around. Most weekday mornings, Elisabeth went to a little preschool located inside our building for a couple hours. After class, we met other stay-at-home moms and their little ones at the pool for lunch and an afternoon swim. Those days were filled with sunshine, laughter, and large plates of the world's best chicken fried rice.

I should probably mention that when I found out I was pregnant, Frits asked me if I wanted to get married right away. I commented that it wasn't part of the plan yet, but that, *of course*, we should get married before the baby turned two. I randomly threw out that number in the moment. We didn't need marriage to be our moral compass at the time, nor did we feel the pressure so many unwed parents might feel. But my flippant comment ended up coming true.

When Elisabeth was almost 23 months old, we flew to Michigan to drop her off with my mom and Earl, then flew to Hawaii to get married, just the two of us. Getting married in Hawaii had always been a dream of mine. When I was a young girl, my grandparents traveled to Hawaii and brought back a picture of a cute little chapel on a cliff overlooking the ocean. After seeing the picture, I knew *that* was the kind of wedding I wanted to have someday. When Frits and I first started dating, we found out we had this in common. We were in no way talking about marrying each other early in our relationship, but we realized that he, too, had always dreamed of getting married in Hawaii! So that's what happened.

Ten days after our private wedding on the beach in Maui, we returned to my parent's house to pick up Elisabeth. My mom threw a lovely reception to celebrate with our family and friends. It never occurred to me that perhaps my parents didn't appreciate our small intimate wedding without them. Maybe they wanted to be invited, too. But it was already over. Frits and I shared the wedding of our dreams.

In the years after getting married, Frits, Elisabeth, and I moved several times. We returned once again to the Netherlands, but this time to a larger city called Eindhoven. Elisabeth was three years old, and I was newly pregnant with Harrison. Adoption was still a possibility and a dream, but I admit that my maternal instincts kicked in, and I convinced myself I needed another baby. And adoption wasn't an option while we were still moving around so much. Even a home study, a necessary part of the adoption process, would have been impossible. We knew our time in Eindhoven, Netherlands, would be short-lived due to Frits' consulting assignment, which soon required a move back to the US. I gave birth to Harrison just two months after we moved from the Netherlands to Mountain View, California. During my stateside doctor's visit at 37 weeks, I tested positive for eclampsia. Harrison's heartbeat was dropping much faster in utero than we expected, and my blood pressure was going through the roof.

I had to be induced. After he was safely delivered, Harrison spent the first few days of his little life in the NICU, similar to Elisabeth. Except that this time, I needed to stay in bed in my own room while my new baby was across the hospital.

On the first day, the nurse called my room to tell me that Harrison was ready to be fed, so it would be a good time to come down. I tearfully told her I couldn't come down to the NICU (doctor's orders as my blood pressure was still too high) but asked, *"Could you bring him up here?"* She sweetly told me that wasn't possible, but she would send a picture. Soon a polaroid photo was delivered to my room. I think it made me feel worse to see my little boy connected to tubes and wires, lying there all by himself. Still very medicated, I started having dreams that Harrison could walk by the time I got to see him. Harrison was in my dream, still newborn-sized, walking around like an adult, wearing a diaper with all of the monitor wires dragging behind him. I was a bit of a mess, but the dream was short-lived. The next day I was allowed to go to the NICU to see Harrison. Two days later, we were a family of four—all home together.

Thankfully, both of my babies turned out to be healthy and strong with some extra medical care in the first few days. Fast forward twenty-plus years—our daughter Mia gave birth to her sweet little girl, Kira, who would also need to spend her first few days in the NICU following a very difficult delivery. After traveling the world, meeting women in Haiti, Guatemala, and Uganda, and hearing their stories of not having access to the most basic medical care, I feel extremely grateful and determined. I'm grateful that my first two babies and Mia's baby had the medical care they required when they needed it the most. It also made me aware of what is required to help other women around the world afford decent care for themselves and their babies.

Now on the West Coast with our two little kids, we loved that Frits could choose consulting opportunities based on wherever we wanted to live. So we made one more job transfer from Mountain View in northern California to Valencia in southern California. We had the best communities wherever we lived, and moving around had its perks. There were always fun places to explore, and we became the destination vacation spot for friends and family who wanted to come for a visit. My favorite memories of being a young mom were those days living in Valencia, just outside of Los Angeles.

But life wasn't without its challenges.

I never did go back to school to finish my degree. Moving around so much made it hard for me to find work I felt passionate about outside of our home. And then there were friendships. It was hard to make long-term friends when I knew our proximity would be short-lived. But I made the most of it, and I still had my lifelong friends from 6th grade to carry me through the times when moving around got hard. In fact, I still see those friends—Marne, Marie, and Tiffany—several times a year.

If there is a bit of advice I can give women of any age, it is to cherish your friendships. Our spouses, partners, and families become all-consuming in certain seasons, but there is something magical about having other women in your life. I mean good women who lift each other up and cheer each other on. The best friends are those that love you at your worst but believe that you are amazing and have so much to offer the world. There's also something beautiful when women come together to accomplish a common vision. We would see more of this magic in the years to come.

Another hard part of moving around so much meant I had to put my desire to adopt on hold. It was hard to complete a required homestay when our addresses and acquaintances kept changing. After we had Harrison, I looked into foster care and local adoption. I came across some material from Help One Child in Los Altos, California, and started following the work they were doing on the West Coast. Their premise was that if everyone fostered just *one* child, the world would be a different place. I loved this thought, but our almost-transient lifestyle made local foster care a challenge. For one, most agencies require that you live locally. And second, Frits worked a lot, and I was the one taking care of the kids most days. Through Help One Child, I learned about what would possibly be required to foster children: travel, parental visits, court dates. Under these circumstances, foster care felt close to impossible. That's when I started looking more seriously into international adoption.

Now, I want to pause here and say that I'm very aware of the privileged life I've led. In all those years of moving to different parts of the US and the world, I sometimes had help to clean my house or do our laundry. I usually even had help with my kids if and when I needed it. But the truth is, I didn't always feel fulfilled. I spent a lot of mental energy looking for the "next big thing" where my passion and my purpose would collide. And yet, even in the middle of my search, I still loved the opportunity to pick my kids up from the school carpool line and tuck them into bed every night. Especially when Frits was on the road or out of town. I know things would have been quite different if I had to work full-time to help put food on the table. But Frits did this for us. I loved every single moment of it! At the same time, I often longed for something more, as many of us do.

In 2002, I found out that a few of my sister Jen's friends from back home in Michigan were going to the Mother Teresa Orphanage in Haiti to volunteer. They asked if I wanted to join the trip, and I immediately said *yes*. Sara and Sarah were the leaders. They shared some information with me on the phone since I had missed the preparatory meetings required for the rest of the participants. Little did I know that the situation I was walking into in Haiti was about to blow me away. The purpose of my first trip to Haiti was to serve, but I also had an ulterior motive. I wanted to explore the idea of international adoption, and this was the closest experience I had on the calendar.

I flew on the red-eye from Los Angeles to Miami, then eventually to Haiti to meet up with Jen's friends in Port-au-Prince. Even waiting at my gate in Miami was a cross-cultural experience. All around me, people were speaking Creole. The plane ride to Haiti was the first time I remember being in the minority. As a late twenty-something white woman, it was strange to have traveled all over the world and never felt this way before. I remember some of the Haitians around me ignored their seat assignments and sat wherever they wanted, a feeling that was a little unnerving for a rule-follower like me.

During the flight, I was reading a book about Reactive Attachment Disorder (RAD) because I wanted to know what I was getting into if this adoption idea was for real. The book seemed to be a "worst-case scenario" description of adoptees with RAD, and I was rattled by the stories of children trying to stab their adoptive parents. When I landed in Haiti, I noticed men with machine guns lining the rooftop ahead and waiting by the rolling stairway that would allow us to disembark the plane.

Between the book and the machine guns, I felt my confidence slip away. As we descended the airstairs and proceeded into the tiny immigration room, it was completely packed shoulder to shoulder. Bodyguards pushed several of us aside to make way for a small, well-suited man. Most people seemed to recognize this man, but clearly, I didn't. When I asked the person next to me who the man was, he pointed to a photo on the wall for reference. *Ah, President Aristide.* No wonder crowds and military men were waiting for him in the sweltering heat. At that time, I had no idea of the giant atrocities this man of small stature had committed during his time in power. Aristide's government worked hard to improve the education and medical system for Haitians, but the human rights abuses of anyone who spoke out against him were severe. A year or so later, while in a very long line at the airport, I had a conversation with a Haitian man. Somehow we landed on the topic of limited access to birth control for women in Haiti. In reference to Aristide's government, I said something about "how ridiculous" it was for birth control to be so limited. The man immediately shushed me and looked around to see who might have heard me.

After what seemed like hours packed into the extremely hot baggage claim area, my suitcases full of donations arrived. I made my way out of the airport into a sea of people trying to carry my bags to make extra money. Among the chaos and intense heat, Sara spotted me and shouted over the crowd. I made my way towards her, and we loaded my luggage into a small tap-tap—a little pickup truck with a makeshift roof over the bed, wooden benches, and no seatbelts. A large, jovial Haitian man drove us to the guest house where we were staying. Sara and I made it back by dinner. The rest of the team had arrived a few days before me, and they did their best to mentally prepare me for what I would see. However, as I was about to find out the next morning, their preparation wouldn't be enough. When the sun rose, we walked fifteen minutes on a dirt path next to the busy road and crossed over a bridge. Underneath, there was a river of trash with puddles of water where women were washing laundry, and their children were picking through the garbage next to pigs and goats. I learned a bit about life in Haiti just on the walk to the orphanage. But I was so grateful to be there and had a strong sense this would be a turning point for me.

When we arrived, I was surprised to see that the first floor of the orphanage was a hospital. I was introduced to the handful of Sisters who worked in the orphanage and hospital. The head nun was only a few years older than me and from Lima, Peru. The women wore long, white sarees with three blue stripes around the border and looked beautifully regal. After I spent a few moments with the nuns and could see past their iconic clothing, I realized these were fun, spunky women just like my friends and me. They were real women who loved each other and every child in that building. But I needed to wrap my head around the reality of what these women were dealing with each day.

The Mother Teresa Orphanage was founded by the Missionaries of Charity Center in Calcutta under Mother Teresa herself. The Calcutta center was established in 1950 to provide support to those in need. And since its foundation, the order has expanded and now comprises 4,500 nuns in more than 600 missions across 133 countries around the world.[10] Quite orderly and impressive!

That first morning, I stood in the middle of rows and rows of emaciated babies in clear acrylic bassinets on rollers. I was scared to death to touch a single baby. The hospital was a sea of sick babies in dire need of daily medical attention who only got to see their mothers or family members once a week during visiting hours. And unless a group like ours showed up to help, these babies spent most of their days laying in those beds crying, only to be fed and changed when necessary. On average, there were 25-40 babies *per nun*. That's a lot of dirty diapers and bottles to prepare! And the reality was most of these babies were malnourished and needed NICU-level care.

It was our "job" to be the Sisters' extra hands. They had so much to do and didn't have the luxury of one-on-one time to hold these precious babies and coax their tiny mouths to drink just a bit more.

It took hours to slowly feed a few of the babies who were so weak they could only take one tiny sip of a bottle at a time before needing to pause and rest. We changed dirty cloth diapers and dirty sheets. I stayed focused with the thought that every diaper I changed was one less diaper a Sister had to take care of, freeing her up for more important tasks. The nuns did the best they could to keep things clean, but there was so much going on at any given time.

On the second floor of this hospital was the orphanage with children ranging in age from just a few weeks to about ten years of age. These kids had so much energy to expend! Keeping them occupied was a full-time job for the nuns looking after them.

During the hours we worked at the orphanage, I watched as young women, older women, and even a few men dropped off their babies and small children for care. And I wondered, *will they be back? Will they be able to care for their own children once they receive the medical attention and nourishment their little bodies so desperately need?* Visiting hours were the best and the hardest to watch. Once a week, one family member was allowed to come back and visit with their child at the hospital. If the child was doing well, the parent or caregiver could take the child outside of the hospital grounds as long as they brought them back once visiting hours came to a close. Watching one young mom wipe tears from her eyes as she checked her baby back in at the hospital was one of the hardest things I had ever experienced up until that point. It just wasn't fair. I know the reasoning was that many of the parents were not healthy themselves, and the policy was there to limit additional exposure to disease for the incredibly sick children. But it was still unsettling that I, the white lady from America, got to stay with their babies while they had to go home. I'll never forget how it felt to hold those precious babies while praying that God would allow them to live.

Mesi Jezi—Thank you, Jesus!—was the common phrase we heard when parents showed up the following week during visiting hours to find their child was still alive. I remember one mom who showed up to see her baby, not only alive while I held her in my arms, but her baby was starting to thrive. She shouted *Mesi Jezi!* and started crying, dancing, hugging me, and thanking me before scooping her baby into her arms for a few hours of visiting time. That's when I realized that these mothers didn't even know what had been happening all week. They had no idea what kind of condition their babies were going to be in when they arrived again, some of them having traveled hours to get to the hospital.

After the second day of volunteering in the orphanage, I was quite confident that my emotions were in check and that I could handle whatever the day held, no matter how hard. But when I walked through the double wooden doors and saw the babies all lined up in their plastic bassinets, I had a new realization. I realized how much pain these babies must have been in because they were literally starving to death. My eyes instantly filled with tears. At one point, with nowhere to hide inside the cement block walls, I turned my back on the room, buried my face in my hands, and sobbed. It was all so much—too much—to take in. Very much against my will, my emotions overflowed. I was so mad at myself. It felt so selfish and weak to cry out in the open like that. One of the nuns came to check on me. She wrapped her arm around my shoulders and kindly asked, "What's wrong, dear?" I thought, *What do you mean, what's wrong?!* I took a few deep breaths, wiped my face dry, and tried to smile. I assured her I was fine and proceeded to care for more crying babies. Those nuns were so impressive. They worked hard every hour of every day in one of the hardest places to live and serve I could possibly imagine.

I still remember one particular baby from that trip. Her name was Jennifer. It was obvious Jennifer was more of a toddler because of her height, yet she weighed no more than twelve pounds. Jennifer lay lifelessly in the middle of her tiny bed all day, even when she was being changed or fed. Sarah noticed me watching Jennifer and told me it was okay to slow down for a bit and simply hold her for a little while. When I picked Jennifer up, she barely moved, and I could see bruising and discoloration all over her frail body—signs of being severely malnourished. With her discolored skin and sunken eyes, she probably should have at least three IV drips. But there she was, free to be held by me. Sarah sat next to us, holding a baby or two on her lap as well. I tried feeding Jennifer, but it was a slow process. She was almost unconscious as she took slow and tiny sips from her bottle. At one point, I looked over to respond to something Sarah said when I felt a fly land on my cheek. I went to swat it away, but thankfully, I turned my head and realized it was Jennifer reaching up to touch my face. She was awake and aware of what was going on! I looked into her huge dark brown eyes as mine filled with tears yet again. My chest ached for this little girl. Our eyes met for a moment before her eyes closed and she went back to taking sips from the bottle I was holding.

This was a turning point for me. I was drawn to serving these sickly babies. I knew there was a desperate need for more places like the Mother Teresa Orphanage and people like the nuns, and even a need for more people like me. At that moment, it felt as though I was looking into the eyes of Jesus, and he was asking if I was willing to keep serving him and "the least of these."[11] It was one of the most profound moments of my life. I had never felt such a connection to God. It was a feeling of such sadness and heartbreaking love, and yet at the same time, purposeful hope. I still can't tell the story of Jennifer without crying, but I do know that sweet baby had much more of an impact on me than I ever could have on her.

After four long days working at the orphanage, I flew back to the US. Sara and Sarah stayed the rest of the summer and called me a few weeks later to tell me that Jennifer was doing better. I was amazed. She was so sick, yet with the most basic care and supplies provided by the nuns, Jennifer eventually went back to her mother. She could now grow into a little girl.

I flew from Haiti to Michigan for one of my closest friends, Marie's wedding shower before heading back home to LA. It felt like complete culture shock to go from holding babies in an orphanage just a few hours before to a fancy bridal celebration. Everyone kept asking the question I had no answer for:

"How was your trip to Haiti?!"

While I appreciated their care, I kept saying,

"I still don't know."

I needed time to process my experience, and a wedding shower was not that kind of time and space. When I got back home to California, I found my way back to my routine. I was happy to be with Elisabeth and Harrison again. It took a few weeks, but soon I started processing my experience out loud—first with Frits and then with other friends, including my sister, Jen.

I am a problem-solver, solution-seeker, action-taker kind of girl, and I had just stumbled upon a gigantic problem that needed solutions. *A lack of orphanages and an overwhelming amount of orphans in Haiti.* The hardest part was that the situation felt dire. There was no time to waste, and there was a desperate need for more help in Haiti for orphaned babies who needed urgent care. That was the first problem. (I look at this much differently now than I did 20 years ago.)

And the second problem was personal for me: I still couldn't shake the idea of adoption. Deep down inside, I felt we were supposed to adopt, and I had a feeling our future son or daughter would be from Haiti. One day when the topic of adoption came up, I told Frits that we either needed to go for it or forget about it, but staying somewhere in the middle was no longer an option for me. He agreed.

Because we weren't practicing Catholics, we couldn't adopt from the Mother Teresa Orphanage, but I knew they weren't the only orphanage with children needing homes. I trusted my instincts and knew this was what it had to be. I knew our next step would be adoption, regardless of how dangerous or complex the options seemed. (Granted, I say that now, being clueless at the time about the danger and sadness ahead.) So, in a matter of weeks, I was booked on a flight back to Haiti. Not only did I have this strong maternal instinct to adopt, but I knew deep down inside there was more I could do to help—more we could *all* do. All I needed to do was pay attention to my instincts and trust my gut.

Chapter Three

··········

HOPEFUL CHARITY

Do What Only You Can Do

I COULDN'T GET HAITI OFF OF MY MIND. Those babies, those nuns, those families dropping off their sick kids in need of dire care, and those children running around the orphanage. I had gone from needing to look at a map just to find Haiti to having Haitian faces forever imprinted on my heart. After I started processing my experience out loud with Frits, I had two things on my mind: adoption and a return trip to Port-au-Prince. The first would prove more challenging than I anticipated, and the second would happen again within a matter of months.

In the coming weeks, I spent my free time looking up websites of American orphanages in Haiti. I figured they offered the fastest adoption process for welcoming a new son or daughter into our home. Elisabeth and Harrison were now in elementary school and preschool, which meant my time was my own for a few hours every morning. And this was how I spent it, scrolling online. One day, while looking at a nonprofit Haitian orphanage website, I came across a picture of a little girl named Sophia. She was just a few months older than Harrison, and my heart did a little flip inside. *That's her. That's the daughter we're supposed to adopt.* A few weeks later, after several phone conversations, filling out applications, and talking with Frits, I purchased airline tickets to meet Sophia in person. We started the home study process by gathering the massive amount of required paperwork. All of a sudden, things started to feel very real.

I traveled back to Haiti that fall (September 2002) with other adoptive parents. We were all scheduled to meet the children we intended to adopt for the first time. (Little did I know the tiny baby girl we would eventually adopt had been born only one year before that trip). When we arrived at the orphanage, I couldn't find Sophia in the sea of children, which concerned me a bit. Carla, the American woman leading the trip, was introducing children to their adoptive families. When she realized I was still standing there by myself, she checked with the orphanage staff and found out Sophia was actually at another orphanage. This seemed a little strange. Carla made some phone calls and pretty soon, Sophia was brought to us. I'm still not sure what was going on, but I felt really uneasy.

When I met Sophia, I knelt down on my knees and stretched out my arms. She gave me a big hug and then ran off to play with her friends. She was so happy to see them. Sophia was a tiny three-year-old with a spicy personality. I adored her right away. I spent the next several days playing with Sophia and the rest of the adoptive parents and their children. I started learning little things about her. She loved playing in the water and "reading" books. She loved spaghetti but hated avocados. She was sweet and cuddly, and you could tell she just really wanted "a person." *She really wanted a mom.* I wanted to be that person for her. Every morning, Sophia's orphanage would bring her to the American orphanage, where we would spend the day together before she returned to the Haitian orphanage to sleep. I was told the Haitian orphanage was run by a local female pastor. It sounded okay in theory, but I wasn't so sure everything was fine. I called Frits several nights to update him and ended up crying on the phone. Even though Sophia and I had a delightful few days playing together, I felt uneasy about the situation. And then it was time to go home.

As hard as it was for me to leave Sophia, I understood that this was all part of the adoption process—a process known to take one to two years to get through all of the adoption bureaucracy and legal requirements. Frequent trips would just have to be my reality if I wanted to see her before she came to live with us in our home.

I was back in Haiti one month later, in October. This time I traveled with Vanessa, an American woman I met through my new friend Carla. Vanessa was an adoptive mom from Chicago. She had a huge family and a huge heart. Vanessa had been traveling back and forth to Haiti to help several orphanages by bringing much-needed supplies and volunteering her time. Orphanages were always in need of diapers, formula, basic medicine, and extra help. Vanessa was a well-practiced mama who had better knowledge than most of how to help with malnourished babies. And she had a good relationship with the female pastor who ran the orphanage where Sophia slept at night. On this trip to Haiti, Vanessa was bringing more supplies to the pastor's orphanage. She also planned to visit the child she was in the process of adopting. I really felt that if this adoption with Sophia was going to go through, I needed to travel with Vanessa to meet and befriend this pastor. I was told she was not getting the necessary paperwork to the American orphanage for Sophia's adoption, and I thought maybe if she knew me, it would help.

I called my mom and asked if she'd be willing to come to California and watch the kids while I was gone. She agreed, took a week off work, and hopped on a plane to California. Frits was going to be busy at work, so it was comforting to know she would be around to pick up Elisabeth and Harrison from school. Plus, she would get to spend some special "grandma time" with them.

The night before I was scheduled to fly to Haiti for the third time, I had a huge bout of fear like never before. And it scared me a little. Okay, actually, a lot. I kept hearing the warning of a tiny, internal voice of fear. *Don't get on that plane tomorrow, Gretchen!* This overwhelming feeling was with me throughout the evening, even as I kissed the kids goodbye and gave my mom a big hug on my car ride to LAX. I just couldn't shake it. Sitting in the waiting area near my gate, getting ready to board my plane, I almost tossed my $750 ticket in the trash, turned around, and went home. But I just kept thinking about Sophia. If I didn't go, something told me I would never see her again.

When it was time to board, I stood up and made myself walk down the jetway and onto the airplane. I found my seat, sat down, put my seatbelt on, closed my eyes, and let out a sigh. And just like that, the fearful feeling evaporated. It was almost like the feeling had lost its power once I committed to getting on that airplane. With no more work to do, it disappeared. I often think about that moment because if I hadn't gone on that particular trip, there would have been no Three Angels, and today there would be no Trades of Hope.

Vanessa was waiting for me when I landed in Port-au-Prince. We were both excited to get to the pastor's orphanage with our supplies, and I was extra excited to see Sophia. I could tell the pastor liked us by her welcoming presence and warm hospitality, and we really liked her, too. She even invited us to stay with her in her home.

Before we got to her house, Vanessa and I stopped by a different orphanage for disabled children. Vanessa had a contact there, and she was considering helping the house manager who was, understandably, always in need of supplies, donations, and extra hands for care. While Vanessa was talking to the sweet little grandmother who ran the place, I met one of the board members who was also there for a visit—another American man. I told him why we stopped by and mentioned I was interested in adoption. Our conversation was interrupted by an invitation to lunch with Vanessa and the older woman. So we hopped into a tap-tap and headed to a local pizza place. While Vanessa and the woman were immersed in their own conversation in the front two seats, I sat across from the American man in the back of the tap-tap. (Essentially, we were sitting on benches in the back of a little pickup truck.) At one point, our eyes locked, and he leaned forward and said quietly,

"You need to walk away from this place right now and not have anything to do with this woman. I'm here as a board member, and the embassy is getting involved in the situation and will be pressing charges soon. She is purposely making the children sick. Walk away."

I nodded yes to acknowledge that I understood what he was saying without drawing attention to the seriousness or severity of our conversation. We made small talk over lunch, and then Vanessa and I dismissed ourselves to head to the other Haitian orphanage to meet the female pastor. I filled Vanessa in along the way. We did walk away from the situation, trusting the board member was being an advocate for those vulnerable kids.

When we got to the pastor's house, I was surprised to see she lived a very upper-middle class lifestyle (more *upper* than *middle*). It matched her larger-than-life personality, so I didn't think too much about it beyond my initial surprise.

The orphanage she ran, also where Sophia lived, was not what I expected compared to her house. While her home was modern by all Haitian standards (even US standards), the orphanage was another story. It was rundown and in need of so many repairs that I lost count as I eyed the property. I couldn't bear the thought of what it must be like for Sophia and her friends to sleep there every night when I had a clean, comfortable bed waiting for her at home. And at the time, I just couldn't comprehend why the adoption process in Haiti took so long, especially when there were parents like us eager to welcome these children into our homes in the US.

Back at the pastor's house, we met a young girl whom she referred to as her niece. But I quickly suspected there was something strange going on. This is when I first learned about children known in Haiti as *restaveks*, although I wouldn't learn the term nor what it meant until later. Essentially, this girl was a child slave. She appeared to be 10 or 11 years old—it's so hard to tell with children who are small and possibly very malnourished. There were a few other clues that made it obvious she was something other than a family member living in the house. On Saturday evening, she prepared a meal for everyone, which she served but never sat down to eat (clue #1). She delivered cookies and milk to the pastor and her husband later that night as they settled into bed (clue #2). The next morning, I saw her carrying water in five-gallon buckets into the house so the pastor's husband could bathe and shave (clue #3). That Sunday, we all went to church to hear the pastor preach, and the little girl stayed behind to do housework (clue #4). It was apparent she was responsible for cleaning the whole house, even sweeping the leaves off the dirt driveway. Those were chores only a restavek would be asked to do.[12] Her sleeping quarters were in a small building outside with a simple cement floor (clue #5). She may actually have been a niece, but she was also their servant. And my heart dropped. Vanessa's did, too.

The pastor was so warm, vivacious, and happy...until that Sunday afternoon when she realized we knew her truth. Not only did we realize the truth about the child slave in her home, but we knew the truth about where all of the donations for the orphanage seemed to go—her own pockets and her lovely home. I really liked her up until this moment. And then I didn't know what to do.

Days before this, I ended up giving the orphanage $800 for new mattresses because the current ones reeked of urine. What child wouldn't opt to pee in their bed instead of using the filthy outhouses late at night, which were actually just holes in the ground? But I got to see Sophia, and that made it all worth it. I remember bringing a baby doll as a present for Sophia. She loved that little doll right away, but the first thing she did was remove the doll's hat—the *chapeau*—and shove it in my pocket because she didn't want any of the other kids to take it. I still have that tiny pink hat. Sophia seemed concerned that the doll didn't have *sandeles*. She kept pointing to the doll's feet and asking, "*Sandeles? Sandeles?*" I shook my head "no" to break the news that her doll didn't come with sandals or shoes.

My worst suspicions about how the pastor ran the orphanage were confirmed when we realized the supplies we had brought to the orphanage two days earlier were no longer in the pantry where they belonged. On Sunday afternoon after church, we went to the orphanage, intending to help in whatever way was needed. And, of course, I was really looking forward to seeing Sophia. We were shocked to find there were no adults in sight. Just kids running free and wild. When Vanessa and I showed up, they ran to greet us and motioned for food. The infants were all crying and laying in dirty diapers. It seemed no one had been there all day to take care of them. Vanessa called the pastor and left her a voicemail. We were certain she would be furious when she found out her employees had abandoned the kids all day. We got to work taking care of the kids until we heard from her. After breaking into the padlocked pantry, we found very little food left on the shelves. (Breaking into the pantry felt very rebellious and empowering at the same time!) So we made do with what was left to get these kids fed, including the crying babies who needed their bottles. It was the first time I ever cooked over an open fire in a big cast-iron pot. Luckily, Vanessa knew what she was doing and started the fire to make oatmeal while I mixed the remaining formula. *What were the employees doing with the food supplies we brought just one day earlier? Were they using them as their own or selling them for money? Who would steal from these children?!* We will never know.

That afternoon while Vanessa and I fed the kids and changed their diapers and their bedding, the pastor showed up with a young, plain-clothed policeman who had a handgun tucked next to the badge on his belt.

"You have no right to be here on a Sunday!" the pastor said, with the policeman giving us a stern look.

We were dumbfounded.

Vanessa was not one to back down from a situation where justice was warranted. Things got heated quickly between Vanessa, the pastor, and the police officer. He was armed, and we were standing in the middle of nowhere.

Sophia was still wrapped tightly around my neck as I took a step closer to where they were standing. I surprised myself and screamed at Vanessa,

"Shut up!"

It had the effect I hoped. Everyone stopped, and Vanessa and I knew this was our cue to exit. We were not going to win this fight.

I gave Sophia one last squeeze as I pulled her arms off me and handed her to one of the older girls. She sobbed. With tears in my eyes and an attempt at a reassuring smile on my face, I said goodbye to Sophia. I knew I would probably never see her again.

Vanessa and I both broke into sobs as we left in the back of our tap-tap and drove down the dusty dirt road. We were only three days into our trip to Haiti and had already witnessed two dysfunctional orphanages. I also realized by this point that the first American orphanage I visited was corrupt in its own way as well. (Although Carla, the woman who led my first trip to meet Sophia, was so very kind and supportive.) Not to mention the loss of my dream of adopting Sophia. It wasn't just that we couldn't adopt her. It was knowing that she would most likely live in squalor her whole childhood. My chest ached and my head throbbed. Vanessa and I were both devastated, but for different reasons.

Vanessa asked our tap-tap driver to take us to a restaurant she knew. It turned out to be a beautiful little European restaurant near the pastor's house. The restaurant sat behind cement block walls with a huge iron gate, and we showed up unshowered and filthy. I thought the hostess might send us away, but she showed us to an outdoor table where we sat under beautiful trees full of twinkling string lights. It was lovely, yet felt utterly ridiculous. How could something so beautiful exist in the same place as Sophia's orphanage? We ordered *steak frites* (steak and french fries) and sat quietly for a few moments. We were both so exhausted. And between the two of us, there were no more tears left.

Out of my exhaustion rose a sense of resolve. I knew my choices: *either walk away from Haiti or do something about what I saw.* A new idea emerged.

Over dinner that evening, Vanessa and I started talking about opening a home for infants—a small orphanage in Port-au-Prince to serve more orphaned babies in need of care. I felt so strongly that God was calling me to do this. It was my way of making a difference with what I knew up until that point. So, I dug for a pen in my bag, and when I found one, I wrote down a few thoughts on some scrap paper. Vanessa and I turned those thoughts into a plan. She was just the friend I needed that night.

After dinner, we walked back to the pastor's house to pick up our bags. The road we walked was pitch black, but that didn't stop Haitians from walking the road late at night, too. It was so strange hearing their voices but not being able to see anything. I guess this is one of those things you adapt to when street lights aren't accessible. When we got to the house, the pastor and her husband were waiting inside. It was awkward, to say the least. We quickly grabbed our stuff and waited outside for Sonia and Michel to pick us up. I had not met them yet, but Sonia and Michel were friends of Vanessa's from her work at the American orphanage. I was so relieved to get in the back of their car. On the ride to our hotel, I felt a deep sense of determination. I had a few short days left in Haiti, so I had to move fast if I wanted to get started with our plan. (The people I work with today know this about me better than anyone: when I'm resolved about an idea, I take action. There's no sitting around and waiting. I value when people lead with their actions over their words.)

The plan: *a new orphanage for orphaned babies in need of care.*

The first step: *find people I trust to get started on the ground with the work right away.*

I reached out to a few people, some of whom used to work for the American orphanage (the one that led me to Sophia). I wanted to provide quality care for up to ten babies at a time, which meant finding Haitian staff I could trust, and fast fundraising once I got back to the US.

My next hurdle: tell my husband that I think I'm (we're) supposed to open an orphanage in Haiti to take care of little babies. I couldn't find a way to ease into that conversation well. So as soon as I got home, the first thing I blurted out was,

"Honey, you want to open an orphanage with me?"

I really had no idea how he was going to respond. He paused, looked into my eyes, and said,

"Sure."

He could tell by the look on my face that I was already there. He's been so supportive since day one.

Less than three months later, at the beginning of January 2002, very little money had been raised. I was still trying to figure out how to gather donations, connect with churches, and ask people for their input on the plan. Grief started to surface, too. If I'm being honest, it took me a few months to accept the idea that Sophia would never be our daughter.

Since our first conversations in Haiti, Sonia and Michel were on board to work with us. They were already looking for a property and building in a good location that met our needs. Maxon, who had also worked for the American orphanage at one point, was a huge help. I met him because he was the person driving Sophia back and forth between the orphanages. I liked him from the first time I met him. And he was so sweet to Sophia. Everyone involved in the project agreed that this initial discovery process and the gathering of support and funds would take at least six months. But six weeks into planning, Maxon called to say a woman had just begged him to take her new baby. The newborn was so premature that she fit into the palm of Maxon's hand. The mother told Maxon her milk hadn't come in, and she was sure the baby was going to die. We offered to help buy formula, but the woman had several children, and she didn't believe she could care for this tiny baby. So, Baby B (as we'll call her here) was in need of immediate care, and without a place to provide that care, Maxon reached out to a network of women he already knew who were hoping to become nannies. Baby B was the first infant in our care; two more babies—Andy and Mia—would follow. This was the "official" start of Three Angels! The original group of nannies took care of the first few babies in their own homes while we supplied the essentials: diapers, medicine, formula, and bottles. These caring women were our very first employees.

A few months later, Maxon found a property that suited our needs. It was a large two-story home with three bedrooms. The house was owned by a Haitian woman who was now living with her family in the United States. It was in great condition with a stone facade and hand-carved wooden cabinets in the kitchen and every bathroom, and there was a lot of room for little ones to run about. This would become the site of Angel House orphanage and later include a school and medical clinic.

Maxon and a young man named William were our first house managers. Maxon organized the nannies hired to help with infant care, and William lived on the property with his wife and young son. While they were getting the right people in place, Vanessa and I were pulling together a ton of supplies, including cribs and mattresses from the US, to fill the house. We traveled to Haiti that spring and brought furniture, mattresses, and hundreds of pounds of supplies with us to open Angel House on the first day.

As we launched our nonprofit charity in Haiti, I traveled back and forth quite a bit. The rhythm I eventually settled into was flying to Haiti every five weeks for five days at a time. This allowed me to oversee operations as necessary and make sure our team had what they needed to care for these sweet babies.

It was also my time to be with the little girl we ultimately adopted, Mia. I was able to get to know her spunky personality. I learned that she loved to eat ice, and there was no way I was getting her to drink milk, only water. She was so cuddly and loved to be carried everywhere.

At 18 months, Mia pretty much ruled the house with half a dozen babies. Her tiny size made it quite entertaining to watch her demand so much attention. As she bossed them around, the nannies would just laugh at her. Mia would often play with a toy telephone, talking away in Creole. One day, she was talking on the phone, laughing, and telling a very animated, very long story. I asked Maxon what she was saying as I knew about ten words of Creole at that point. He told me she wasn't saying anything. She was just rambling. That little girl had such a playful, joyful personality. And I was smitten with her.

Mia fixing my hair, helping her nanny and talking on the telephone.

Here are a few more stories that come to mind as I think about those early days at Angel House orphanage. This is a brief recap of who and what shaped my heart and mind towards charity as a necessity in those days:

BABY B

Baby B needed immediate care, so we hired the nanny to care for Baby B in this woman's own home. The nanny fed her the nutritious formula she needed and provided around-the-clock care. And a miracle began to happen—*Baby B grew*. A few weeks later, once she was strong and steady, we took Baby B back to her parents to show them how well she was doing. We told the family that we were happy to help them care for her (providing formula and check-ups) and wanted them to have the opportunity to take her back. With a hopeless look in their eyes, they showed us where they lived and told us about their family's situation. They already had so many children and not enough food. And they still didn't think they could care for Baby B well. So she stayed in our care for eight years until she was able to go home with her adoptive family.

MIA

The day Maxon told me about Mia via email, she was almost 18 months old. Mia's birth mom lived in Cite Soleil, generally regarded as one of the poorest and most dangerous areas in the Western Hemisphere.[13] It was essentially a gang-ruled shanty town of approximately 300,000 people. With canals in the streets as the primary sewage system and corrugated homes with dirt floors, it wasn't hard to imagine how difficult it would be to keep a baby healthy. Mia was malnourished, and her mom said she was sick often. After much consideration, Mia's mother dropped her off with Maxon. He emailed a picture of Mia to me that day and said, "I found your daughter!" In the picture, Mia was sobbing. My heart broke looking into her sad eyes, knowing she must have been so scared. Maxon knew I planned to adopt a little girl, and he sensed this particular little girl was meant to be a part of our family. I was trying to trust that God would bring the right little girl into our family, so I took this as a sign that she was the one.

Once Maxon found the property where we established Angel House, I flew down to Haiti. It was May 1, 2002. Maxon and William brought Mia and her nanny, Madame Dauphin, to meet me at the house we were renting nearby. Madame Dauphin was carrying her, but as soon as Mia saw me, she went straight into my outstretched arms. She buried her face in my shoulder, looked up, and smiled. I knew at that moment with my whole heart she would eventually be a part of our family.

A BABY & HER GRANDMOTHER

One day, an elderly woman showed up with a tiny newborn in her arms, begging for help. As she held the baby out for one of us to take, the grandmother told us her story through tears. The baby's mother—her daughter—had died the week before, and the grandmother was trying to keep the baby alive. But it was obvious to all of us, including the grandmother, that the baby was starving to death. The baby—who didn't even yet have a name—was alert but so thin. It had been impossible for her grandma to find medical care for her. Knowing what I know now, there was a good chance that all this dear woman needed was formula and a bottle. But in the moment, I knew we were not qualified to care for this tiny little girl, yet we had no connections to reliable medical care. She really should have been in a NICU with doctors and nurses caring for her, which wasn't available at that point anywhere in Haiti. We were a last resort for this grandmother and her sweet baby granddaughter. The staff at Angel House, along with myself and a few friends who traveled with me to help, took turns holding the tiny little girl, feeding her little bits of formula throughout the rest of the day and night.

The next morning, as we were getting dressed and ready for the day, my friend Gail was holding the little girl while she took her last breath. We all cried and prayed for the baby and her grandmother. As was customary in Haiti, two staff members took her to the morgue— one to drive and one to hold the baby. I wanted to ride with them to hold her on the way, but they told me the morgue was in an unsafe area and didn't want to put anyone else in danger. With eyes full of tears, we all watched the truck drive through the orphanage gates until it disappeared.

Less than an hour after the men left for the morgue with the baby, her grandmother came back to check on her. My heart dropped when I saw her walk through the gate. I had to tell her that her granddaughter had passed away earlier that day and had already been taken to the morgue. I felt dread in my stomach as I knew I was about to break her heart. Someone brought her into the office, where I joined her. We sat in the only two chairs positioned across the small room from each other.

In broken Creole, with a translator standing nearby, I told her I was so sorry, but her granddaughter passed away very peacefully that morning. Her face crumbled from sadness. I walked over to her, bent down to hug her, and we both burst into tears. I held her thin body tight against mine. She smelled of perspiration and urine, but I couldn't have cared less. The more she cried, the longer I held onto her.

It was hard to tell how old the grandmother was—she looked quite elderly, but I have no doubt that a really hard life with very little food does that to a person, too. And now this dear woman lost her daughter and granddaughter just days apart. It seemed so unjust! That beautiful baby would still be alive if this grandmother had access to free formula. It was obvious she really loved that little girl and would have taken good care of her. A few cans of formula and this story would have been so different.

This was when my burning anger started for just how incredibly UNJUST this was. I had little in common with that woman, and yet, in that moment, we were so similar. We loved the children in our care so fiercely and wanted them to be healthy and well. I understood why she was heartbroken even though we didn't speak the same language.

This was when I started realizing that these women—mothers, grandmothers, aunts, and sisters—needed job opportunities to provide for their families so they could stop their children from starving to death or being abandoned.

CHARLES

One morning in Haiti, I was in the orphanage changing diapers, drying and dressing babies as the nannies pulled them out of the bath basin dripping wet. I loved those mornings when everything felt clean and new and hopeful. And I loved spending extra time holding the babies as they drank from their bottles. I'd gaze into their eyes as I prayed that we were giving them the care they needed to develop into happy children. As I sat on an orange child-size chair feeding one of the babies, surrounded by a few toddlers running around the orphanage, one of our employees, Jonathan, came upstairs to get me. He said there was a couple in the office who needed to talk to me right away. I reluctantly handed the baby in my arms back to one of the nannies, stepped over the rambunctious toddlers around my legs, and headed downstairs to the office.

A middle-aged couple sat in the office chairs waiting for me in the sun-filled room. They were well-groomed, yet their clean clothes were worn, and they were both so thin. The man immediately jumped up to give me his seat and stood behind his wife with his hand on her shoulder. I noticed her swollen belly. As it turned out, she was quite far along in her pregnancy. The woman began to share how they had been married for years and used to work as teachers at a local elementary school until the school closed a few years ago. Since then, they hadn't been able to find consistent work. The wife picked up a few sewing jobs here and there, and the husband found occasional work as a day laborer. But those opportunities were not consistent and paid very little. They already had three boys at home. As they talked, their eyes welled up with tears that spilled down their cheeks. They told me how they were unable to regularly feed their current family of five. And they simply couldn't take care of another baby. I felt a few tears spill down my cheeks, too.

Here sat two educated parents who obviously loved each other and their children, telling me they wouldn't be able to take care of their next child. And they were asking if we were willing to take their baby. I was shocked and heartbroken. They looked expectant as I took a long time to find my words. The husband, still standing, held tight to his wife's shoulder while she held the hand he placed there.

This was not the typical situation we were used to at Three Angels. Typically, our staff worked with parents like these two—parents who could no longer afford to take care of their babies—to help find a solution so they could keep their children. Most of the time, the parent in need of support was an uneducated, young, single mother. In these situations, our staff encouraged parents to tell their extended families about their situation, hoping those family members would help be a part of the solution to care for the child. Sure enough, our staff already had this conversation with the couple. They knew it was the first thing I would ask. They knew I would have questioned why we were taking the baby of a married, educated couple without first trying our best to help find a solution. So the staff handled the conversation with this couple on their own until there was no solution to be found. That's when they called me down to the office. And here we sat.

Surely, there must be a better way.

I told the couple we would give their situation some thought. I asked them to keep searching for a solution at their end, too.

The next time I returned to Haiti, I was there the day they came back with their tiny baby boy, Charles. They walked through the gate, up the stairs, and into Angel House with Baby Charles wrapped tightly in a blanket in his mom's arms. He was beautiful. Absolutely perfect, with dark curls and soft little cheeks. She handed him to me with tears streaming down her face. Baby Charles wore a clean white onesie with a sweet little cotton vest handmade by his mom. It was light blue and had a little white dove embroidered on it with tiny white buttons. She told me she had sewn it as a gift for him. She wanted his new mom to know that she loved him. We agreed to take Charles into our care. I was afraid they would leave him with another orphanage if we didn't, and I truly believed we were the best option at the time. But I was praying it was only temporary.

When it was time to say goodbye to his parents, I cuddled him and carried him slowly upstairs to the nursery with a heavy heart. Before I introduced the nannies to the precious little guy, I laid him on the changing pad and unbuttoned his little vest. I knew it would just get lost in all of the other clothing, as would the loving message Charles' mom wanted to send. I gently took it off and carried it downstairs to my room, where I put it in a large ziplock baggie in my suitcase, so I could preserve it and give it to Charles' adoptive mom one day.

What I remember most from that day is knowing from the deepest places in my heart that the whole thing was *wrong*.

I knew it was *wrong* that simply because this family lived where they did, these kind and loving parents didn't have the opportunity to provide even the most basic of needs for their children.

I knew it was *wrong* that these parents felt they needed to give their child away.

I also knew it was *wrong* that this family couldn't handle one more mouth to feed.

And I knew I didn't have any way to help them at that point except to take this child in and find him a new home.

Later that day, sitting on the floor of the screened-in sun porch where I slept on my trips to the orphanage, I cried out to God:

"This isn't right, but I don't know what else to do."

And I remember feeling like God replied:

"You will know what to do in the future."

I don't know why this had to happen to Charles and his birth parents, but I do know it was something God needed me to experience. To me, that day was my Ebenezer stone[14]—a reminder of God's presence and help when I desperately needed it. I could only imagine how Charles' parents must have felt. This experience was such a hard yet valuable lesson for me. It was sobering to realize this very same experience was happening to families all over the world, every single day. I wanted to find a way to *make it stop.*

SPENDY

After Angel House was up and running for several years, we started a private elementary school for kids in the local community. In addition to caring for orphaned babies, education was a priority of Three Angels Children's Relief, our organization. I thought this would be a meaningful way to help Haitian families. US AID studies on education in Haiti from 2020 show that the average Haitian, aged 25 years and older, has had less than five years of schooling. And only 61 percent of the adult population is literate. Poor literacy in Haiti starts early. The same set of studies from US AID conducted early reading assessments on Haitian school children and found that 75 percent of first-graders and 50 percent of second-graders could not read a single word.[15] So, historically, there has been a huge shortage of quality educational opportunities. We hoped to help fill that gap at our school. Every child at our school who needed assistance (more than 50% of the students) received a backpack of supplies donated by our generous friends back in the States.

I'll never forget a little boy named Spendy. His mom dropped him off at Angel House, no longer able to care for him. To this day, I can only imagine the desperation his mother must have felt dropping off her little boy with us. He was a lovable little kid, but she made it clear she could no longer care for him. We enrolled him in school and worked hard to find him an adoptive family right away. But then, Spendy's mom changed her mind. A few months later, she knocked on our front door and asked to take him back home. We met in the office where some of the supplies and backpacks were being stored for the upcoming school year. Spendy's mom said she wanted to take him out of the orphanage but asked if he could remain in our school. "Of course!" I said. I loved this idea because it meant we could continue our connection with this sweet little boy. As we were discussing the school schedule and the need to register with our headmaster, Spendy's eye caught a Batman backpack full of books on the pile by my desk. I picked up the backpack and handed it to Spendy,

"Do you like this backpack?" He nodded his head.

"Then, this is for you!" I said.

He was delighted, and I was thrilled to be able to give him this substantial gift. But the look on his mom's face was a flash of sadness and anger. Our eyes met, and in that moment, I knew. *How much more meaningful would it have been if I had handed the backpack to Spendy's mom so she could hand the backpack to her son?* Another moment when I realized just how much our helping hurts[16] if we're not thoughtful with our actions. Beyond her anger at what I had done, I'm sure Spendy's mom wished she could have bought that backpack for him. But she couldn't, and he needed the supplies.

These experiences made me realize that while we had the best intentions with our charity work, we were no different than other charities offering bandaids to the desperate and dangerous situations families faced in Haiti. Caring for orphans, even if they were poverty orphans, was a real and tangible need. And we were meeting that need. But providing care for these babies was just a bandaid over the gaping wound of poverty. Most of these children had strong, capable, loving mothers who just needed opportunities and resources to take care of their families. We were operating a hopeful charity, but it was only a fresh bandaid on an old wound. *Something had to change.*

FLORIDA

In 2006, we moved from Valencia, California, to Palm Coast, Florida, so I could travel to and from Haiti a lot more. Mia's adoption was finalized in 2004, so she finished preschool in CA and started kindergarten in Florida. Frits had started his own consulting business at this point—thank goodness because we spent a few years living what felt like separate lives with all of his work travel and my time in Haiti and at home with the kids. Plus, we knew deep down inside that we wouldn't be in California forever. The East Coast just made sense. I could easily get to Haiti and see my family in Michigan and Florida, and Frits could fly to the West Coast just as fast as he could fly home to the Netherlands to check in with his family.

My friend Shannon was still involved with Three Angels as well. She offered to maintain Three Angels connections between our church community in Valencia while we established new connections and found a home church in Palm Coast. Between Shannon, Frits, myself, and our board of directors in the US, we made sure the other half of our team in Haiti had the supplies and materials they needed. We sent contractors to build the additional buildings we needed for the school and the medical clinic that my sister Jen would eventually help establish. We also started a sponsorship program for the orphaned babies in our care. Those days of transition were filled with a lot of phone calling and fundraising. Our church back in Valencia was so generous to Three Angels, even after we moved. And for that, I will always be grateful.

I thought I would travel to Haiti from Palm Coast a lot more than I actually did. By that time, we had two house managers living at Three Angels—a retired couple from the US. They had things running smoothly (or so it seemed), so I started spacing out my trips from every five weeks to every three months. This is a decision I would later regret.

With more time for reflection between trips, I felt a growing discontent over the way we were "helping" Haitians. *Were we really helping them if families couldn't stay together?* I wasn't so sure anymore.

Elisabeth, Harrison & Mia finally together in California.

Chapter Four

NAVIGATING CHANGE

Look Beyond the Bandaid

IN FIRST GRADE, I FOUND OUT I HAD DYSLEXIA. My teacher, Mrs. Wrynn, watched as I slowly started falling behind the other kids. My reading progression slowed down while other kids were speeding up. I still remember the way I felt on the day I got bumped down to the middle reading group: *horrified.* I ugly-cried when Mrs. Wrynn told me. Now I had two things to be embarrassed over—slow progression and a public demotion. After failing a few spelling tests, she told my parents I needed to get tested. I'm not kidding when I say Mrs. Wrynn saved the trajectory of my life. Because I was diagnosed with dyslexia at such an early age, I never really fell behind. Of course, there was some initial catching up I had to do in first grade. I struggled off and on throughout the rest of elementary school, and whenever I did, I went to a tutor. Truth was, tutoring was kind of fun! Keeping up with my classmates fed into the confidence I already had from a steady, secure home life and a mom who always told me I could be and do whatever I wanted—even though many years later, she would say she had her doubts. (Parents, just keep those kinds of thoughts to yourself. Let us all live in our happy place of thinking you thought we were capable of anything—no matter our age!) My early childhood dreams were to be a lawyer or a dance teacher. I loved the idea of bossing other people around and wearing fancy clothes. And I've always loved dress-up and fashion. Thank goodness that later in life, I realized there were easier ways to dress up than becoming a lawyer!

THE SCHOOL

When we had the opportunity to open a school at Three Angels, I knew it was what we needed to do. There were little girls all over the world who needed caring educational support like I had in my teachers, tutor, and family. And I loved the thought of being able to create that kind of intuitive and fun learning environment with our Three Angels team. We started by providing schooling for the orphaned kids in our care. Vanessa, who was still involved with our team, met an American Greek Orthodox priest, Father Michael, who ran an elementary school in Haiti a few years prior. He always seemed like such a great man. He taught me a bit about being Greek Orthodox and, over pizza one evening, assured me one beer a day was both medicinal and necessary for dealing with the parasites that came with living in Haiti. (Very unprofessional medical advice, but it was funny coming from him.)

Father Michael died of a heart attack one day, and his family back in the States didn't want the responsibility of the school. They sent word to shut it down. Vanessa met with Alix, one of the teachers at the school. He asked if we'd be willing to consider taking over the school. Father Michael owed a lot of back rent, so we couldn't just take over the property. But Alix was passionate about helping us keep the school open for the remaining students, and we had another vacant building on our property at the orphanage. As they closed the doors to Father Michael's school, we opened the new school on our property. Alix was not only willing to continue teaching at our school, but he also stepped in to function as headmaster. He figured everything out. Kids were enrolled in school, families were told about the transition, and the school was registered with the government.

We called the school Three Angels Christian Academy. But after we registered the name, Alix told me it didn't translate well into Creole. So, everyone just called it Taca (TACA), which to me always sounded too close to caca (Spanish for poo). Haitians could be both respectful and direct, but this was one of those times when I wished it went the other way: direct, then respectful. I really wished I could have known about the poor translation ahead of time, and we would have called the school something different. But we didn't, and the name stayed.

The building itself was small for a school, so we had to get creative. We followed the French educational system that is common in Haiti, which meant our preschoolers started school at age 2.5. Preschoolers through 2nd graders came in the morning, and 3rd through 6th graders came in the afternoon. The school-age children at the orphanage attended the school, but most of the children were from the surrounding neighborhoods. The little ones were so adorable coming into school each morning. I always tried to be in Haiti during the school week rather than on weekends. And I loved watching as the little ones played on the playground dressed in their uniforms each morning before they gathered to sing the national anthem and raise the Haitian flag. Alix taught them two Sunday School songs in English, "This is the Day" and "When the Saints Go Marching In." If any Americans were helping out at the school on a weekday, they would sing along. I often wondered which songs they sang when we weren't there.

It wasn't uncommon for the two and three-year-olds to fall asleep towards the end of their first few days of school. The teachers would just pick them up and lay them on nap mats we had brought over from Angel House. No matter the grade, the students came to school with huge backpacks, wearing uniforms a few sizes too big to allow for growing room. At times, we were able to provide an English teacher at our school, and it was very sweet to hear the little ones learning basic English words such as "please" and "thank you."

I was so thankful for the opportunity to start the school. Had it not been for the foundation laid by Father Michael at the school he ran until his death or for Alix, we would have never been so successful. I knew school was one of the safest places for these kids to be, especially the girls. Extending any kind of education for young girls beyond their primary years was no small feat in and of itself. Many families wanted their girls home to do household chores and cook meals. But often, these girls became young mothers, and without the ability to read or write or do simple math, *the cycle of poverty* continued. This was another thing that broke my heart. I saw these problems of poverty, but the only thing we could do was encourage these girls (and their families) to stay in school.

Some of our children came from homes where they could afford to pay a small amount to send their kids to our school. Every state-run school in Haiti has tuition costs, and Alix shared that we needed to charge *something*; otherwise, it wouldn't be perceived to be a quality school. So, at the beginning of the year, some parents contributed to the tuition, and scholarships supported the remaining costs. We willingly accepted their small fees because it meant other children without means were covered, too. By the end of the school year, everyone was on full scholarship.

School fees went towards things like school supplies, teacher salaries (which we supplemented with donor support), building upkeep, and uniforms. We even provided white, fluffy socks and hair ribbons for the girls. I learned my lesson in Haitian fashion through those hair ribbons. Our uniforms were navy blue bottoms with white button-down shirts, so I thought it would be cute to provide yellow hair ribbons with white polka dots. This did not go over well with the Haitian mamas, who insisted that yellow and white did not match the blue uniforms. On the first day of school, I didn't understand why not one of the little girls was wearing the yellow hair ribbons we handed out. Every ribbon was white! Alix explained to me that the yellow and white polka dots didn't match the navy and white uniforms. Well, that explained the strange looks I got from the moms the previous week. Once again, it showed how much I had to learn about Haitian culture and fashion preferences with things such as colorful hair ribbons.

Alix was the reason our students thrived and our school won academic awards. He started a feeding program so all our kids would have lunch provided for them during the school day, even if it was a simple peanut butter and jelly sandwich in the beginning. For some kids, this was the only meal they had all day. By the first day of school, Alix knew every single child's name. He was amazing. Later, I learned he spent the whole summer before the start of the school year conducting house visits to interview the children and get to know their family situations. His dream was to one day set up schools all over Haiti. And my dream at the time of writing this book is that Trades of Hope will eventually be able to help him do just that.

THE CLINIC

A few years after the orphanage and school were up and running, we decided a medical clinic was a good addition to our growing umbrella of charitable aid and relief. And we still had a little bit of space on the corner of our property where the clinic would fit perfectly. We just had to build it.

My sister, Jennifer, initiated and led this project (technically, she was my step-sister, but we never acknowledged the "step" part and always skipped straight to just being "sisters"). Jennifer is a nurse practitioner, and she had a friend and nurse-midwife colleague, Linda, who also agreed to help. Linda had just lost her teenage son, Aaron, to cancer. So Jen and Linda cast the vision for the clinic and raised the necessary funds to build the clinic in honor of Aaron's life. Aaron's photo and a dedication plaque still hung in the clinic the last time I visited. We named it Three Angels Medical Clinic. (I know, *very original.*) A team of people from Michigan and Florida, along with my family, came to Haiti on a week-long trip to build the medical clinic. A young man named Rob was a construction contractor, so he helped us build the clinic according to US construction code standards. I'm so thankful we did. It was the one building left standing without the need for repair after the earthquake. At the time of the building trip, Harrison was in 4th grade and loved working alongside Alix, who showed up in his work clothes each day to help with the physical labor. Alix and Harrison became fast friends, and it was so nice to see my worlds colliding.

In the years after the clinic was finished, Jen and Linda spent many hours working there on frequent trips to Haiti. They brought other doctors, surgeons, and specialists to treat people alongside them. They treated many of the staff, students, birth parents, and families at Three Angels, but they kept a few appointments open every trip so people from the community could sign up to be seen and, hopefully, treated. We had a Haitian school nurse at Three Angels Christian Academy named Clotilde. Every time my sister came to town, Clotide worked extra hours at the clinic for a few days. She also helped Jen train returning groups of US medical staff who took turns coming to the clinic on medical mission trips. One time, I saw my sister drain a huge cyst from under a young woman's arm. The woman said it was really painful every time she moved her arm. After the cyst was drained, she cried and thanked Jen. I never considered going into medicine, but at that moment, my admiration grew for my sister. I had a bit of envy that I couldn't help people the way she did.

To this day, I am really grateful for the work we got to do together at Three Angels over the years, and I am truly in awe of the way she helped people heal from their wounds. Even when we weren't in Haiti, Jen and I would talk almost daily about the clinic and what was going on at the school and orphanage. I miss having regular contact like that and working with her on something so purposeful. My desire to maintain closeness with Jen after we closed our time in Haiti was part of the reason we eventually bought a small summer cottage in Michigan. We wanted to be near my parents, siblings, and their families.

THE STAFF

Once all three entities were up and running—the orphanage, school, and medical clinic—the tension we had to manage was to remind everyone connected to Three Angels Children's Relief that the orphanage was our main priority. Education and healthcare were necessary, but they came after our mission to meet the most basic needs of the babies and children in our care: *food*, *water*, and *shelter*.

And we were able to meet those needs because of the kind staff we had on the ground in Haiti.

While William and his family were our very first house managers, when he was offered a job in the Bahamas, we asked our friends Sonia and Michel if they would be interested in the live-in house manager position. They were a Haitian couple who picked us up from the pastor's house in the early part of my story and continued to offer support and advice over the first years. I had gotten to know them and considered them good friends. They were supportive of us, friendly to the nannies, and so kind to the babies. They said yes, and we watched as they grew their family over the years, now with two little boys. I really loved working with them until we learned they were pocketing extra funds donated to the orphanage.

I arrived at the house on one trip to Haiti, so happy to see Sonia. I went up to the apartment that was connected to the orphanage. It was where all of our house managers lived on the property. I saw Sonia, and as I was hugging her hello, she said,

"Just so you know, I bought those ceiling fans with my own money."

Um, okay.

I thought that was weird, but whatever. I hadn't even noticed the two ceiling fan boxes stacked on the balcony. I knew they were saving and gradually building a house a few miles away. Later during that same trip, we realized the books weren't adding up correctly. Michel was an accountant by trade, and while he had another full-time job, he also worked part-time for us, helping with our records at Three Angels. I knew I had to have a difficult conversation with Sonia and Michel about the missing funds. I was so sad and hurt to realize there had been intentional mismanagement of money coming into the orphanage, and I knew we had to let them both go. It was hard to part ways, but it had to be done.

We also had several American house managers. First, there was Angela. The kids all called her You-you for some reason. We found Angela in a way that I can only say was simply "divine." I was sitting in a tiny booth at a restaurant called Elephant Bar in Valencia, California, having lunch with my friend Tracy. I showed her the stack of photos I had just picked up after being developed at Target. (Yes, this was the early 2000s, and we still "developed" photos.) Our waitress, a blonde curly-haired twenty-something, asked about my photos as she refilled our waters. I told her they were pictures from an orphanage in Haiti that I had started, and I had just returned home after my latest visit. The waitress said she had always been interested in helping with something like this and asked if I'd be willing to meet up with her sometime to talk about it more. We always needed more help, so Angela and I met a few days later and talked for hours. She asked lots of questions about the work we were doing in Haiti. I really enjoyed my time connecting with her. Shortly after our meeting, she decided to move to Haiti and become our new house manager. The day I met Angela, I had just returned from Haiti on the very same trip where I had to let Sonia and Michel, our previous house managers, go. It was divine timing, and I was so grateful!

I traveled back to Haiti with Angela to get her moved in and situated. I introduced her to the staff and some of the locals we interacted with on a regular basis. The kids at Angel House immediately loved her, and she loved them, too. One night we were sitting in the house manager's apartment at the orphanage when she told me a "divine" story. As she was packing to leave for Haiti, she got to the bottom of her dresser drawer and found a slip of paper that read "Three Angels Children's Relief in Haiti." That's when she remembered a friend of hers, Brendie, who heard about Three Angels from a local newspaper article in Valencia, California—the town where we all lived. Brendie gave the clipping to Angela the year before, knowing she wanted to find an organization like ours. Angela had completely forgotten about the conversation until she found the slip in her drawer while packing for Haiti. Angela was our house manager for the next few years until she decided it was time to move back home to California.

When Angela left, Sandy moved in. Sandy was in her 70s and was such a firecracker (meaning she had more spunk and energy than most of us combined). Sandy saved everything because "you might need it!" She had a reputation for fixing and reusing everything and was a no-nonsense kind of woman with the biggest heart to serve everyone around her. I met Sandy because she went to church with one of our adoptive parents, who lived just south of me in Florida. I'll never forget the day we met for lunch. Sandy chose the restaurant: Texas Roadhouse in Daytona Beach. I knew within the first five minutes of meeting her that she would work well as our next house manager. After a background check and a short interview, she was on her way to Haiti. Just like I'd done with Angela, I traveled with Sandy to get her settled in. I loved our late-night chats in the house manager's apartment when she told me stories about her days as an RN and working in the Peace Corps. Decades earlier, she had lived my dream! Sandy met her husband while serving in the Peace Corps and had such fun stories about the two of them. She told me a story about riding a motorcycle across the deserts of Afghanistan to visit her then-friend, who was a doctor. They fell in love, moved back to the US, and had a family. When I met Sandy, she had already been widowed for several years. And the Sandy I knew was always busy serving, helping, and living her life very purposefully. Both she and I thought her time with Three Angels would be short-term, but Sandy still works with Three Angels to this day and has managed their guest house in Port-au-Prince for many years.

Then came Mitch and Monica.[17] They were a retired couple from the US. Monica had been a nurse, and Mitch had been a doctor for nearly forty years. If I remember correctly, they reached out to us via our website and said they were interested in serving in Haiti in some capacity. I remember getting a call from Shannon after she talked with them, saying something like, "You *have* to talk to this couple. They are amazing and would be great to manage the orphanage!" Mitch and Monica were the reason our records were in such order at that crucial moment after the earthquake—when the embassy required all of our paperwork so our kids could get their humanitarian parole visas. They kept the orphanage in tip-top shape, but their relationships with the staff and the surrounding locals left much to be desired. In hindsight, I learned a few hard and valuable leadership lessons while they were managing the orphanage. But at the time, I knew nothing except what seemed to be their excellent operational care.

CHARITY VS. DEVELOPMENT

With great house managers in place over the years, I eventually started spacing out my trips to Haiti. When we moved to Florida, I thought I would take more frequent trips to Haiti, but it wasn't nearly as necessary anymore with Mitch and Monica on the ground. Traveling back and forth now seemed like an unnecessary expense. That's also when my family needed me the most. Parenting teenagers was hard, especially when it involved helping one of our kids process the trauma of abandonment and adoption. Not that I feel I did a great job at it in hindsight, but home was where I needed to be. And I could ease my questioning conscience about spending more time at home because the Haitian children were in good hands.

Still, I had a nagging wonder if the work we were doing in Haiti was somehow wrong. If there were still women showing up to drop their babies off at the orphanage because they could no longer feed or afford them, *were we actually helping, or were we perpetuating the problem? Were we just putting a big fat bandaid on a gaping wound?* During this time, I read another book that rocked my world called *When Helping Hurts* by Brian Fikkert and Steve Corbett. Honestly, I put off reading it for a few months as I knew it might make me regret decisions I had made while working in Haiti. But, in the end, this book helped put some of my uneasiness into words. The authors talked about how so many well-intentioned people and charitable organizations actually hurt more than they help without even realizing it. They talked about the importance of connecting with the locals as much as possible when working in another country. They encouraged charitable organizations to employ local labor for building projects to create more jobs, but also because those locals have expertise and insider knowledge. Locals know where to get supplies and how to get things done in their own country.

I started to think of ways we had "hurt" the local economy more than we "helped" it in Haiti. One obvious way we hurt the local economy was by bringing teams of US contractors and laborers to build the medical clinic. While I'm still glad we followed US building codes, we could have employed more local tradesmen. There were other examples all around us, too. At one point, I heard how a US church donated a huge container of peanut butter to be handed out in Haiti. But Haitians actually make their own peanut butter on a daily basis. It's one of the few products made and sold by small business owners without having to import it. There was also a popular "one-for-one" shoe company shipping containers of shoes from the US to Haiti when there were local shoemakers and cobblers on almost every corner around Port-au-Prince. These generous donations were helping a few in the short term, but in the long term, they were most likely hurting the local economy.

Another example hit close to home. When my kids were little, we put together shoe boxes full of small gifts for kids in developing countries through a Christian organization known for delivering those boxes during Christmas. Then when I was in Haiti, I heard some Haitians talking about how the Americans just showed up and gave their kids shoe boxes full of stuff without asking them if it was okay. They didn't understand why we thought it was so important that their kids had "stuff" for Christmas. For many people around the world, random stuff wasn't what Christmas was all about. The truth was many of the shoebox gifts ended up littering the streets. For some of the parents, it wasn't a welcomed gift. It was more of an intrusion. We thought we were helping, but now I know that some of our charitable gifts were actually hurting.

There was also the time when an American family came on a mission trip to Haiti to serve with another local charitable organization. They hit it off with one of the boys in the school, and when they learned how far he walked every day to school, the family insisted on buying him a bike. The head of the organization politely declined their offer, but the family insisted, and the boy ended up with a shiny new bike. Of course, he was thrilled with the new bike, but it made his neighborhood friends jealous. As the boy rode his bike home from school on the first day, he was beaten up by a bunch of older kids alongside the road, and they stole his new bike.

After watching those Save the Children commercials as a child, I always thought charity was the answer to making the world a better place. I thought it was the best way to help other people. But after several years of running Three Angels Children's Relief in Haiti, I learned so much and realized I didn't see the kind of change I would have expected. We were constantly responding to the tyranny of the urgent—just trying to make sure kids were *surviving* with warm beds and a bottle full of formula or a plate full of food so they could make it through the next day. But what I really hoped for were families who were *thriving*.

Here's what I believe to be true after my experience running a nonprofit in Haiti for eight years:

Most charities are bandaids.

Charity is a necessary and temporary fix to big problems like natural disasters, famine, war-torn communities, and abusive situations. Charity gives people helpful resources such as relief aid, education, and contributions to development as a whole. But when those contributions aren't given with the local community in mind, they're just bandaids.

If this rubs you the wrong way, please hear me out. There isn't anything wrong with donating your time, resources, and energy to things you believe in, but charity isn't always the best solution. Charity doesn't solve the problem of global poverty, of mothers not being able to keep their children. Not long-term, anyway.

There are so many things we, as Americans, think we know about the rest of the world. We think we have the answers to other people's struggles. But after spending time in other places around the world, such as Haiti, I realized how much we still have to learn and how much we may never truly understand. I firmly believe we won't learn important things about how to help solve problems in other countries unless we're willing to listen, pay attention, and look further into the future at the effect of our present-day actions. I knew we needed to navigate change if we were going to look beyond the bandaid with the work we were doing at Three Angels.

This doesn't mean I wish we hadn't started the orphanage. I'm still proud that we helped almost 140 babies and children over eight years without prior experience running an orphanage. Likewise, I didn't know how to start a school, but we did anyway. I'm still proud of how we filled a gap when Father Michael's school closed as we stepped in to make sure over 150 orphans and local children were educated each year. I'm still so very proud of the charitable work we did through Three Angels Children's Relief. This work made a difference for everyone involved in giving and receiving care through the organization. I just wish I had looked beyond the bandaid and navigated the necessary changes a little sooner. It was this charitable work that made me realize there was still more work to be done. Now we had to find a way to make the work more sustainable.

What became more clear to me in those last few years at Three Angels was that economic and social development were the pathways to long-term, sustainable change. That kind of development could positively affect generations to come. And I set my mind on figuring out ways to shift our charitable efforts to sustainable development rather than charity as a bandaid.

Chapter Five

EMBRACING FAILURE

Keep Your Eyes on the Future

TWO WEEKS AFTER THE EARTHQUAKE on January 12, 2010, I had a conference call with our board of directors. I was still recovering from our whirlwind experience of bringing all the kids to the United States, and I told them I was ready to launch a microfinancing program. We talked through the demolition that needed to happen with our fractured building at Three Angels. But we knew it would take years for anyone to be available to do this. Ultimately, the Japanese UN workers came in and knocked everything to the ground with their excavation equipment. Even though construction plans were far into the future, the board agreed to support my decision for us to pursue microfinancing. They also decided unanimously (minus me) that they wanted to re-open the baby care portion of Angel House. My immediate thought was,

"Um, no way. I've already done that!"

Thankfully, whatever came out of my mouth at that moment sounded a bit more diplomatic (I think). Knowing Three Angels would be in good hands with the board and my friend Shannon giving oversight, I decided to do the best thing for them and me.

I resigned.

I felt a wave of relief and sorrow wash over me. Three Angels had been my passion for eight years. It was the place where I found so much of my purpose and I was connected to so many people I loved. I was so sad to leave and end this season of my life, but I was proud of myself, too. Proud of how I stood up for what I thought was best in that moment. The easier thing would have been to put my head down and focus on rebuilding the orphanage at Three Angels, but I knew the commitment and weight of having an orphanage meant I couldn't focus on what I really wanted to do—*help mothers keep their children.* I know those board members also did what they thought was best, and I've always respected them for that. My views on charity had shifted, and I felt that continuing the same kind of work in Haiti would still just be a big bandaid. But it was now their decision to steward, not mine. Just like I anticipated, Mitch, Monica, and Shannon stepped in to rebuild Angel House. And today, Three Angels still has a thriving baby care program for orphaned babies, a school, and a clinic in Haiti.

In the weeks following my resignation, my heavy feelings of sadness and loss became lighter. It felt good to actually do what seemed like the right thing to do. But I had to work hard to redefine failure in my mind. No one was saying straight to my face, "Gretchen, you failed by not going back to Haiti to rebuild and reopen that orphanage."

But I knew there was potential for people to think, and perhaps, believe it. This was yet another time I was thankful for that Michigan girl grit that was still a vital part of me all those years later. When you grow up believing you can be anything and do anything, I'd like to believe that it's easier to shrug off what other people might consider failure. *Was it a failure to provide necessary care to sick and dying babies for the past eight years? Or a safe place for youth to go to elementary school? Or a medical clinic staffed by well-trained doctors and nurses?* Absolutely not.

My only regret is that we didn't find a sustainable solution to the problem of poverty orphans and the plight of those women and families who gave up their babies to be adopted someday. That was where I wanted to focus my time and energy moving forward. It was the right thing to do. This vision filled me with such hope. But first, I needed a few weeks to regroup.

After I packed up and mailed the boxes of necessary paperwork to the team at Three Angels, I imagined a few weeks of domesticity. Cleaning out closets, spending more time with my kids (who were now 15, 12, and 9), catching up with friends, and making slow meals with Frits in the kitchen while we dreamed about our next season. Frits was used to me being away at times and very focused on Three Angels, so this was a change and transition for him, too.

BANKER TO THE POOR

With more space to think and dream, I was reminded of what struck me so hard the first time I read the book *Banker to the Poor*.[18] Author Dr. Yunus does a beautiful job painting pictures of women working hard in a variety of ways to take care of their families. However, because of their harsh circumstances and lack of opportunities, those women were never able to break out of the cycle of poverty. He tells a story about a 21-year-old woman named Sufiya who weaves bamboo stools to sell each day so she can buy food for her three small children. Yunus found Sufiya one day sitting on the dirt floor of her hut with her unclothed children close by. He learned she didn't have the money needed to purchase the bamboo itself, so she borrowed all 22 cents per stool from a local lender. By the time Sufiya paid for the materials, including the interest the man had charged for borrowing the money during the day, she only made a 2-cent profit. Two cents was not enough to feed and clothe her children. So the cycle of poverty continued for Sufiya day after day. Living in the slums of Bangladesh, she could see no other options.

The book gave me a glimpse into a world very different from how I had grown up. Many of these women had been told their whole lives that they brought only misery upon their families because their families couldn't afford the marriage dowry associated with having daughters. Women like Sufiya were told they were nothing but another mouth to feed. But life changed for these women when they had *real* jobs with *real* profit margins so they could provide for their families. For these women, having microlenders—people with financial means willing to invest in their business ideas—meant that someone else valued the work these women created with their hands and their minds. They were more than just their dowry. They were business owners, entrepreneurs, and providers. For a woman to make a viable income meant she was free from so many of the circumstances of poverty that held her down and kept her feeling small in the first place.

I loved reading stories of the women in Yunus' book and imagining their transformation in my mind as they started growing and blossoming into the women they were created to be. I wanted to be a part of creating these kinds of opportunities for other women, too.

Another woman Yunus wrote about named Mufia also lived in the slums of Bangladesh. She was married off at age 13 to a fisherman. When her husband went fishing for long bouts of time, her mother-in-law physically abused her and only gave Mufia small portions of the meals she cooked for the rest of the family. When Mufia's husband returned from his fishing trips, he beat her. She eventually had three children after enduring several miscarriages. Her situation was so horrible that a village leader noticed and offered her a divorce (not a common practice in Bangladesh at the time). She was freed from her abusive marriage, but then what? Mufia was completely on her own as a young divorced woman left to beg in the streets to feed her three young children until another woman took her under her wing and taught her how to weave baskets and mats from bamboo. Through this woman, Mufia was introduced to Yunus and his microlending office at Grameen Bank. She was given a loan and a basic business education from the bank so that she had the materials and knowledge needed to sell goods and save money.

Microfinancing literally saved the lives of Sufiya, Mufia, and their children. I have no doubt those children, now young adults, have had a different trajectory because of the micro financing business opportunities that helped their mothers create sustainable jobs.

What struck me the most about their stories was this: *those mothers and children got to stay and live their lives together.* This could be the solution for women in Haiti, too—women like Charles' mom, for whom the problems of poverty seemed so big and unsolvable, even as an educated woman.

Reading Dr. Yunus' stories and seeing examples of them first-hand taught me the immense power of women being able to earn their own income. By doing so, these women could afford to get out of horrible circumstances and ensure their children were fed, safe, and educated. These women now had a voice and opportunity to choose how to create a better future for themselves and their families. And *that* was the kind of legacy I wanted to participate in.

Even though we had more than enough work to do at Three Angels, my mind was constantly racing with how to help create jobs for the Haitian women who showed up to drop off their malnourished children. How could I help those women keep their babies, provide for their families, and break free from the cycle of poverty?

The answer would eventually lie in *job creation*.

A WALK ON THE BEACH

After we moved to Florida, I found a new friend named Holly, who had helped me when I wanted to start homeschooling Harrison for the second half of fourth grade. Holly homeschooled all of her kids, so she gave me some tips and invited Harrison and me into their weekly homeschool co-op. We made plans to take a walk on the beach one day, just weeks after I stepped down from Three Angels. She and her husband, Mike, were one of the local families who showed up at the Fort Pierce airport to welcome us home after our rescue flight out of Haiti. I knew Holly was a safe place to process ideas for my new dream. I shared about reading *Banker to the Poor* and how I wanted to create job opportunities for women in situations like the mothers I saw in Haiti—women giving their babies up for adoption simply because they didn't have enough money for food. I couldn't go back to doing charitable work if it meant not actively searching for a solution to the problem of poverty. If we could help women alleviate poverty for themselves and their families, we could also help them not be as susceptible to the dangers of realities like human trafficking. Even with years of experience in Haiti, I wouldn't fully realize just how commonplace trafficking was for women and girls for another year or so.

Holly loved my idea of helping other women rise through job creation, and she had some of her own ideas, too. She was a pastor's wife and mentor for other women, and she was an entrepreneur. During a two-hour walk on Flagler Beach, we planted the first seeds of a potential business partnership. In the days that followed, our plan came together. We couldn't wait to tell our oldest girls. Holly and I realized right away that we really hoped Elisabeth and Chelsie (Holly's daughter) would want to build this missional business with us. The girls were on a school trip to Italy that week, so we had to wait until they arrived home to share the news and invite them to be a part of our plan.

This was the moment when all of the ideas I had been dreaming about during our time at Three Angels came to life, and our new business was born!

I was too excited to wait until Elisabeth got home to share the news with her. I knew she was going to love the idea of helping women gain jobs to keep their babies. So, later that day, from the parking lot at Target, I called her in Italy.

"Elisabeth?"

"Yeah, mom. Hey!"

"I have a new business idea for when you get home!"

I filled in a few details, and from that point on, she was all in. And so was Chelsie. Both girls had been taking college classes during high school and would graduate with enough dual credits to earn their associate's degrees at the same time as their high school diplomas. That fall, they were enrolled at Daytona State College, right down the road. So they had fast and easy access to our excitement and, at times, our entrepreneurial chaos. I liked to call it our "entrepreneurial spirit."

While microfinancing was the dream that got me to this point, Holly and I decided on a direct sales business model for our launch. The vision for our direct sales model was that women across the United States had the opportunity to market and sell the handmade products that women around the world were making as Artisans. This way, we could help women have jobs by selling much more than we could ever sell in a brick-and-mortar storefront. It was important for us to purchase goods from Artisan groups so we could build long-term relationships with them. We knew it would take time for sales to grow gradually so the Artisan groups could count on our orders on a consistent basis. This is what allowed our businesses to grow at a sustainable pace together. As our sales grew, their Artisan groups grew, and they were able to hire more Artisans and help more women and their families get up and out of poverty.

If we wanted our idea to be long-term and sustainable, we knew we needed women in the US who understood our mission by selling these products, and we wanted them to earn money from the sales as well. We didn't just want sales volunteers; we wanted sales *Partners*. Holly and I worked for many years with volunteers—her through the church and me at Three Angels. Volunteers were amazing, yet hard to keep long term. Our hope was that if women in the US were earning some extra money to help their families, too, they would continue to prioritize selling products made by our Artisan Partners as their side businesses despite their busy lives. This was the fastest way to get our business off the ground and benefit the women who were making products abroad and the women selling those products. A brick-and-mortar store could only reach so many people, but a direct sales business meant limitless possibilities and limitless impact. We decided to sell fair-trade fashion, jewelry, and home accessories made by Artisans around the world and sold by mission-minded women in the US.

As our sales and reputation grew with Artisan Partner groups, we would hear from the group leaders that women were standing outside their gates each day hoping for a job. The need was so much bigger than anything one person could take on, but we were doing our best to help these women make a difference in their own lives and those of the women around them. There was nothing more beautiful than seeing women helping women *all around the world.*

While we still had a lot of details to work out, I was excited that we had a plan. So many beautiful stories would come from the partnership between the Artisans and the American women selling their products in the years to come.

LOOKING BACK

As excited as I was to move out of charity and into sustainable development with this new business idea, my time in Haiti left an imprint on my heart. It shaped me in unimaginable ways. Standing in front of a child desperate for a mother does something to you. Early on, it stirred the idea of adoption—that is, until I better understood the plight of poverty and these well-meaning mamas who had no choice but to give their babies up for adoption. Then it stirred the idea of family unification, microfinancing, and doing my part to help create job opportunities for those women.

Thanks to Haitian culture, I learned how to be bold, direct, and brave in how I communicate. I learned how to behave in a way that expressed dignity—even when I learned it the hard way—like the time I jumped the long line at the Port-au-Prince airport with $20. A man working at the airport had offered to help me for $20. So I handed him the cash, and he led me to the front of the line. I had no idea what I had done until it was almost over. As I was standing at the counter with the staff checking my bags, I looked back at the sea of faces watching this white American woman cutting in line ahead of them. They were not pleased, and I was horrified at what I had just done. *Never again.*

Without the charitable idea of an orphanage, I would have never learned the lessons I needed to learn, and there would be no Trades of Hope. I had to learn through trial and error, through failure and rebound. And in the midst of it, I realized that sometimes I had to move forward with passionate ideas, even when I didn't have it all figured out.

My one moment of "failure" (stepping away from Three Angels) gave way to a creative idea and a budding business that would be a success in more ways than just the bottom line. I was so excited about this opportunity that I barely slept and couldn't keep my mind off the future.

Three months later, Holly, myself, Elisabeth, and Chelsie hosted a party in my home to sell fair-trade fashion and home goods to our friends. This was the beginning of Trades of Hope.

PART TWO

TRADES OF HOPE

2010-PRESENT

"Work to create the world as it should be."

—BARACK OBAMA

Chapter Six

BEGINNING AGAIN

Repurpose Your Passion & Your Plans

HINDSIGHT IS ALWAYS 20/20.

Those eight years in Haiti taught me a lot of things.
I learned . . .

we are all more the same than we are different,

how to better manage my expectations of others,

that paying more money to get a job done doesn't mean
someone will do a better job,

that people can be happy without hot water and electricity
(but I really like both),

and Haitian church services can last four-plus hours,
so choose wisely.

I also learned a lot about working with expats[19] from the US in Haiti, including several of our house managers. Each house manager lived in the apartment attached to Angel House. It was their job to make sure the property, supplies, staff, and, most of all, the children were well cared for. The house manager was my eyes and ears and my primary contact for everything when I wasn't in Haiti. As you can imagine, each individual brought their own set of skills and passions to the position.

I learned a hard lesson in leadership with one particular set of house managers. We were beyond thrilled they said yes to this position and brought so much experience to the job. But they lacked heart for the mission of our organization, and the hard part was I couldn't see it until it was too late. They had recently retired from the medical field and had all the right skills to run the orphanage. They talked a lot about their passion for serving God and serving others, and they were eager to start helping to take care of our kids. The first few weeks went great. Everything was clean and in good working order under their care. The water pump was fixed, which meant we had running water, something I didn't even know was possible on the property. The kids had personal schedules and consistent healthier menu options for meals, such as hard-boiled eggs, bananas, and avocados—something we tried before but never succeeded in doing consistently when I wasn't there. They organized all of the adoption paperwork and documentation required by both the Haitian and US government. They shopped around to get the best prices for things, which significantly reduced our costs. They stocked the pantry and made sure we had enough water. And they conducted occasional medical exams alongside the school nurse for our students and alongside my sister Jen and the rest of the clinic team for the community.

I thought we hit the jackpot with these two. That is until stories slowly started rolling in about how they spoke to the staff and the kids, even how they spoke to birth parents who brought their babies to our medical clinic and parents who dropped their kids off at the school. There were reports of them not cooperating with the headmaster at the school and not respecting people's property by moving personal belongings from one space to another without notice. These two did *good* work and were literally saving lives. However, they placed more value on how they got things done at the expense of how they treated people. They didn't value people the way they valued accomplishing tasks, and the cracks were starting to show.

For a while, I justified their behavior as the "stress" of living at the orphanage or the "learning curve" of living in an underdeveloped country like Haiti. Then one day, I had a lightbulb moment and thought to myself, *I don't think these two even LIKE the people they're working with!* I kept that thought at arm's length for so long because I wondered, *Who would move thousands of miles away to help people if they didn't even like them?* They were kind and cordial to me, but they treated our team in Haiti as "less than," and that was not okay. Even though they did good work, I knew they weren't the right people for the job. This created tension between myself and one of our board members, who was adamant that I wait until I find their replacement before asking them to step down. In the meantime, the damage done to our community was irreversible. Looking back, I should have trusted my gut and trusted that God would eventually provide someone else to manage the property. But I didn't until it was too late, and it was a hard leadership lesson learned, for sure.

From that moment on, the welfare and well-being of every single person around me was more important than someone's skillset or passion for the job, even if they were fueled by faith. Giving and receiving dignity mattered more to me than pristine floors and well-organized files. Then and now, I truly believe God cares about not just *what* we do, but *how* we do it.

OUR VALUES

I carried this leadership lesson with me as we started Trades of Hope. Selling fair-trade goods in the US would prove to be very different work than running a nonprofit organization in Haiti. But the question was still the same: *How do we always put people first?* That's why, from the very beginning, our team spent so much time talking about values.

After a few whiteboard sessions, we landed on seven values that summed up what was most important to us as founders. These values are still with us today, more than twelve years later:

ToH VALUE #1: We honor God, and we honor each other. On the surface, almost anyone would agree with this idea. But it's another thing to do it day in and day out. It means that there's no room for gossiping or snarky mean-girl stuff, which thankfully, we do not have a lot of at Trades of Hope. We put people first, and we lift each other up. It's my belief that when we're honoring those around us, and we pair it with a genuine sense of gratitude, this is a great way to honor God as well. Honoring each other is the right thing to do. And let's face it, it just makes the world a better place altogether.

ToH VALUE #2: We value collaboration. Not one single person makes this company great on their own. It takes ALL of us together as we strive to listen to each other's ideas and get input and feedback from the home team, our Partners in the US, and our Artisan Partners around the world. We don't pretend to be experts and know everything, but I'm pretty sure *together* we can figure out almost anything.

ToH VALUE #3: We strive to get better. If we want to make a bigger impact, then we need to get better at our business and grow as people. We are always trying to make our products, sales training, shopping experiences, promotions, customer service, and processes for the home team better as we serve our Partners, customers, and Artisan Partners. And we've gotten noticeably good at this over the years.

ToH VALUE #4: We celebrate people. Recognition and appreciation are just some of the ways we celebrate people. No matter a woman's level of participation in Trades of Hope, we value and honor every single person who helps put food on another woman's table around the world. We strive to do this often and well with our home office team, too.

ToH VALUE #5: We value each other's differences. When we all come together, as the women and men of Trades of Hope, we bring our various backgrounds and experiences with us. That's when the magic happens! Regardless of faith or beliefs, economic status, geographical location, race and ethnicity, or gender and orientation, *all are welcome* at Trades of Hope. As we continue to grow as a company, our diverse experiences will only grow deeper, which makes us stronger as a sisterhood (alongside a few brave men) and as a community that cares about making the world a better place for each other.

ToH VALUE #6: We value scrappy determination. This is where our entrepreneurial spirit and positive energy come in. Scrappy determination is about choosing to believe that we have the confidence to make anything work, even when it requires a bit of duct tape and googling answers. It means we don't wait around and expect other people to do things for us. We don't claim defeat because of what someone else did or didn't do for us. We figure things out! As author Marie Forleo says, "Everything is figureoutable." And we believe that with our whole hearts. No matter the size or age of our company, a *scrappy determination* is how we do things. It's how we started in the beginning, and it's how we grow time and time again.

ToH VALUE #7: We believe the best about others. Cultivating this way of thinking is one of the greatest gifts we can give to others and ourselves. Now, don't get me wrong. It's much easier to read into things when we're feeling sensitive about a particular situation. Been there, done that. My friend Holly is the one who actually made me conscious of this. One evening, a few months into our new business, we were packing boxes in the Trades of Hope storage unit. I didn't consider myself a particularly negative person, but I heard myself say, "I can't believe she just said that," and I went on to complain about someone we both knew.

Holly gave this individual the benefit of the doubt and offered a kind response, "Well, maybe she just didn't understand the whole picture of what we're dealing with here." I quickly realized there were a few versions of the narrative I was spinning in my mind that day. To be honest, I was quite embarrassed that I jumped to such a negative assumption about this individual. Perhaps what I believed about her motive was or was not true—I'll never know. What I *did* know was considering the idea that there was an alternative to my story, as Holly suggested, meant I didn't have any icky feelings about the person in question. And I was able to let it go. That was a lightbulb moment for me. When I assume the best about others, I'm a better version of myself. I'm much kinder and gentler to the people around me. And I think it's safe to say this is true for most of us. Assuming the best and choosing positive thoughts about a situation is how we honor one another and ourselves. Bad feelings and unhealthy relationships manifest between us when our actions don't align with our values. This is true for a company, and it's true for every individual like me and you.

YOUR VALUES

Whether you realize it or not, you operate according to a set of personal values, driven by your passions and the skills you've picked up along the way. One of the best things you can do as you look for places to live out your passion and build your plans is to make a list of the things you value. If you're not sure where to begin, a great place to start is to *identify your values*. Your values affect how you and other people make decisions and react to situations. I've found knowing my values helpful in better understanding myself and the people close to me. Here's a helpful *values* exercise for you:

Circle all of the words on this VALUES LIST that resonate with you.

" _____ *is very important to me.*"

ACHIEVEMENT	GRITTINESS	PLAYFULNESS
AUTHENTICITY	GROWTH	POWER
ADAPTABILITY	HAPPINESS	PURPOSE
BALANCE	HARMONY	RELIABILITY
CONNECTION	HEALTH	RESPECT
COURAGEOUSNESS	HONESTY	SECURITY
CREATIVITY	HUMILITY	SELF-DISCIPLINE
CURIOSITY	IMAGINATION	SERVICE
DEDICATION	INDIVIDUALISM	SIGNIFICANCE
DETERMINATION	INNOVATION	SIMPLICITY
DISCOVERY	JUSTICE	SUCCESS
EMPATHY	KINDNESS	TEAMWORK
EXCELLENCE	LEADERSHIP	TRANSPARENT
FAIRNESS	LEARNING	TRUST
FLEXIBILITY	LOVE	UNDERSTANDING
FREEDOM	LOYALTY	UNITY
FUN	OPTIMISM	VISION
GENEROSITY	ORIGINALITY	WISDOM
GRACE	PASSION	WONDER
GRATITUDE	PERSISTENCE	

Now, narrow the list down to ten values . . . then narrow it down to your top three values. Write those top three values down somewhere. Make them visible in a place where you will see them every day. And use those top three values as your filter the next time you create plans or look for places to fulfill your passions and your life purpose.

BEGINNING AGAIN

My plans definitely changed with the start of a new business idea, but my passion and purpose remained the same. I went from taking care of babies in need of life-saving resources to creating job opportunities for mamas so they could provide those resources for their own babies. This was my new plan: *job creation for women.* And here's why: I discovered that when we focused just on the child, as we did at Three Angels, we changed the trajectory of that child's life. At Trades of Hope, when we focus on the mother, it changes not only the trajectory of her life but the trajectory of everyone around her. Studies show that for every woman who works her way out of poverty, she brings four additional people out of poverty with her.[20] And that's the hopeful change we were looking for!

Women in developing countries with job opportunities can now provide food for their families and send their kids to school, which means those kids have a better chance of staying safe and being educated. Those things are not possible for most women who continue living in poverty. Many women in our Artisan Partner groups today are learning more than just how to roll beads and put jewelry together. They're learning how to read, sign their names, and take care of things like inventory management and quality control using Microsoft programs. Several of them are even designing new jewelry over video calls with our team! They went from having very little, if any, money of their own to having a steady job with a livable wage. For many women living in abusive relationships, the abuse has stopped because the men started respecting the women more. As a result, children are now growing up in completely different environments than they were living in before. They get to stay in their families, in their home communities, and in their own culture. And these kids get to go to school there too. This is the kind of ripple effect that happens with job creation for women.

Creating jobs for women was and still is a simple and more holistic way to be involved in alleviating poverty—the problem I had spent most of my adult life trying to solve. But job creation also meant a deep investment in the local community of a particular country, one that would last for a long time. The American mentality of "rushing in to save the day" may work in some situations, like natural disaster relief. But job creation takes more time—more time to learn various cultures and truly understand what's best for women in each culture. I realize as an outsider that I will never completely understand what it's like to walk in the shoes of those women; that's why it's been so critical to involve indigenous people in developing solutions for their own communities. And the truth was, there were already a lot of amazing local organizations in communities and countries doing just that: listening to and learning from the deeply-established cultures of each community.

It wasn't our job to go into a developing community and tell them what kind of jobs we would create for the women who lived there. It was our job to listen, learn, and see what job opportunities already existed and what we could do to help connect local women with those jobs and order more products for job security. Finding a job in or near their existing community was the most sustainable option for women who needed the opportunity. It was also the most sustainable option for us and our business model. We didn't need our people on the ground in every country where we were helping women find work. We just needed to partner with the people already there doing that very thing.

Of course, there are times when our actions at Trades of Hope still look very charitable. We still give financial donations and tangible gifts throughout the year to our Artisan Partners and various non-profits we admire. Gifts include sewing machines, bikes for transportation, freshly-dug wells, and education sponsorships. We call this kind of intentional giving "Gifts of Hope." Our donations go to initiatives that align with our desire to help women rise out of poverty and educate girls. For example, we give to an organization that works in Siem Reap, Cambodia, called 88 Bikes. Their mission is to give as many bikes as they can to girls for safe transportation so that, as they say on their website, *she has a bike that brings her to school, brings her to work, and brings her joy.*

Such a fun day helping to distribute bikes in Cambodia.

Another organization called Mercy for Mamas gives "birthing kits" to pregnant mothers in Uganda. Women in Uganda must bring their own birthing supplies to the hospital, such as surgical gloves, plastic sheeting, gauze, razor blades, and soap. If a woman doesn't have these supplies with her when she arrives to give birth, she can be turned away and denied care (*can you imagine?!*). So, these $7 "Mama Kits" are critical to every woman and baby. On one trip to connect with our Artisan Partners in Uganda, Elisabeth and I had the privilege of handing out Mama Kits to young, soon-to-be mothers in the capital city of Kampala. These women lit up when they held a kit in their hands. I imagine they also felt a huge sense of relief. Those kits represented the best opportunity for a safe delivery. Participating in this kind of giving with my own daughter was one of the best days.

Yes, charitable donations are still part of the way we conduct business. But my motivation has changed. As we like to say at Trades of Hope, the gifts aren't the goal; they are the "sprinkles" on top of the development work we're already doing. And these sprinkles are the small things that make our work so much sweeter. We also make sure gifts are given *in addition* to job creation, not the other way around.

THE NEW PLAN

It seemed the fastest way to create job opportunities for women in developing countries was to work with *established* Artisan Partner groups. And the fastest way to put money in the hands of those women was to purchase their inventory wholesale and then sell that inventory in the US. But first, we had to test the market to see if women in the US would be willing to get behind our mission and vision of job creation for all women as a way to alleviate poverty. *Would they see value in buying goods that were sourced from places approved by the Fair Trade Federation?* There was only one way to find out:

> *Put together a party with fair-trade goods*
> > *made by Artisan groups.*
> *Invite a few friends.*
> *Share the "why" behind Trades of Hope.*

*Encourage women to buy fashionable goods for themselves,
their families, and friends.*

And it worked!

We landed on the name Trades of Hope the same way we landed on our values—with a whiteboard and a few colorful markers. We wanted the name to have meaning yet be fun and not too heavy. Elisabeth, Holly, Chelsie, and I started tossing out words and phrases that came to mind and writing them on the whiteboard in the coffee shop of LifeCoast Church, that Holly and her family started. At one point, one of us called out "Trades of Hope," and it stuck. That was it. I filed the paperwork online later that day for Trades of Hope LLC, and it was official. *We were official!*

At first, I was hesitant to fully engage with Artisan Partner groups until we were sure our idea would fly. I didn't want to get their hopes up for more income if we couldn't follow through with our commitment. While this idea was brand new to us, other companies around the US were selling fair-trade, artisan-made goods from Artisan Partners around the world. But we were one of the first companies doing so with a direct sales model and a mission to create job opportunities for women at both ends of the sales cycle. I knew we just had to try and see.

My friend Megan was staying in our home in the weeks leading up to the launch of Trades of Hope. She had served on staff at Three Angels before the earthquake and was the one who rode on the motorbike to check on the kids right after the earthquake. Megan needed a place to land until she got back on her feet, so she was sleeping in our guest room for a few weeks. One day, she overheard us talking about selling fair-trade goods made by Artisan Partners around the world in a home-party model and chimed right in.

"Hey, I have an idea! What if you purchase through these guys first?"

She held up the Artisan-made journal she carried with her. Her journal was a gift from a family friend purchased in a store called Ten Thousand Villages. We looked up the store, read about their commitment to Artisan-made, fair-trade products, and found out they had a location in nearby Winter Park. So, we loaded up and went to check them out.

Ten Thousand Villages is a company of retail shops that carry unique, handmade gifts from around the world, including fair-trade baskets, jewelry, crafts, and other items from international Artisans.[21] The company was started in 1964 by Edna Byler in the small town of Akron, Pennsylvania. Ten Thousand Villages grew to be a large nonprofit, fair-trade organization marketing and selling handcrafted products made by Artisans from over 120 Artisan groups in more than 35 countries worldwide.[22] We found out we could purchase wholesale fair-trade items made by Artisan groups directly through Ten Thousand Villages as a trial for our idea.

In those early days of business planning, the four of us took care of *everything*, and I mean everything. Elisabeth and Chelsie created our website, complete with photos and all of the content. Holly and I mapped out our business plan. With the plan we had in mind, women in the US would sell our fair-trade accessories and home decor at in-home parties with their friends, who would, in turn, do the same with their friends. All of these home parties would be job opportunities that worked both ways. *Women in the US would make a fair profit selling fair-trade products, and women in Artisan groups would make a fair profit when their handmade goods were purchased upfront by us via wholesale* (meaning the sale of bulk goods to retailers like us). Selling their products wholesale was how Artisan Partners made money.

Their sales weren't dependent on what was sold at our end because we determined what kinds of products to purchase in bulk ahead of time. This would eventually turn into the product development part of our business, but for now, everything was rolled up under one team with one big vision for women around the world.

There were twenty-five women at our first party in September 2010, where we laid out fair-trade, Artisan-made products in a beautiful display and gave our little presentation. We were nervous yet excited! And the best part of all was that because this first group was mostly our closest friends, they gave us great feedback for future home party presentations. Then we hosted another party the next night as we had so many people who wanted to come to the first one, and it went great. After the success of our first two parties, we knew we had something special. Most of the women who attended those parties were mission-minded like us, so they welcomed our presentation on the importance of job creation for women as a solution to alleviate poverty. They were intrigued to learn how purchasing fair-trade goods made by Artisans was a tangible way to create those jobs. Many of these women saw me as a trusted source, having recently run a nonprofit organization in Haiti where I was up close and personal with the damaging effects of poverty on Haitian women. *What mother didn't want to help other mothers feed, clothe, and care for their babies? What woman didn't want to empower other women to be able to take care of themselves?* Convincing these women to purchase fair-trade fashion, jewelry, and home accessories wasn't a problem. They loved the idea. We sold $27,000 dollars worth of fair-trade products that first fall. And we had other women not only asking to host parties but to become sales consultants with us. *We were thrilled!*

That fall, I also read *Half the Sky* by Nick Kristof. It was another eye-opening account of the atrocities happening to women, particularly in underdeveloped countries. Just when I thought I had seen the worst of poverty after living in Haiti, Kristof's stories fueled my passion and made me work on the plan for Trades of Hope all the more.

So much for spending my time cleaning closets.

After a trial run selling Artisan-made goods sourced by companies like Ten Thousand Villages, we found our own pathway to existing Artisan Partner groups and made it a priority to work with and purchase directly from them.

BUILDING A PROGRAM

Eight years into our Trades of Hope journey, Holly and Chelsie would eventually transition out of the business. It was a hard change but a good one. They moved into other seasons and started new businesses with their husbands and remained our good friends. We wouldn't be where we are today had they not been part of those early days.

Holly was a big reason we landed on our direct sales business model early on, and it proved to be working well. When we decided to find our own Artisan Partner groups, I reached out to a few contacts and friends. A friend of a friend, Shelley, was still in Haiti working with a group of women who were rolling beads to create jewelry from strips cut from cardboard cereal boxes. Shelley's mission aligned 100% with ours. She had gone to Haiti to adopt a little boy, much like I had done years before. When she was visiting, she found out that this little boy had a mother. Shelley shifted her focus very quickly. She moved her family to Haiti and started working with just a couple of women in the apartment. Shelley came up with the idea of altering the traditional paper beads you see from Africa to using cereal boxes to roll bigger, chunkier beads. With her artistic flair, Shelley

Gretchen, Shelley, & Elisabeth in Haiti

started designing jewelry that mixed cereal box beads with seed and clay beads to create something new. These women became our first official Artisan Partner group! We purchased bulk orders of the necklaces, bracelets, and earrings they made to sell at our home parties.

The first day we visited this group, we saw Donna Karan, a US fashion designer, there, too. I don't get star-struck easily, but I was a bit giddy over seeing Donna Karan. She was working on a business partnership with Shelley and the Artisans to sell their products in her Manhattan boutiques. Donna's mantra for introducing this fairtrade line into her fashion label was "Inspiring Hope. Creating Change." And that's exactly what we were doing. In fact, I still use those phrases quite often within Trades of Hope. (Thanks, Donna!)

This trip was also the first time Holly and Chelsie had ever traveled to Haiti. The four of us visited the Three Angels orphanage and school. We even volunteered one afternoon at the Mother Teresa orphanage, where I had my first experience in Haiti. It was good to be back, but I was so glad to be with Trades of Hope and no longer running Three Angels. I knew my purpose was to prevent orphans and help mothers keep their babies. Looking around the room, I was sure that most of the babies wouldn't have been there if their mamas had not been so poor—if those women had access to consistent work with living wages.

I was determined for Trades of Hope to be a success, but I was also committed to a self-funded business model so that Frits didn't have to put his own business profits back into it. As the demand for parties and products grew, we needed more space than my living room to organize, sort, and ship products. So we rented a 10x10 foot storage unit for $70 a month. This small recurring payment stressed me out at first. *Would we sell enough products to cover our costs, including the storage unit?* But within a few months, we were busting at the seams and had to upgrade our storage unit size more than once. Now it seems funny that I worried so much about the $70 for rent. But I am glad we were always so frugal.

Cori, Katie, Stacy, Elisabeth, and I were the first "packers." Most evenings, we spent hours at the storage units, packaging and shipping products sold at recent parties. The idea was for our sales consultants, eventually called Partners, to carry only a small inventory of display items, host parties with those items, take orders, and then we would fulfill and ship those orders to the hosts for distribution as soon as the parties were over. This was how we kept our overhead costs down all around. (This was a great way to start, but we quickly realized shipping directly to the customers was a better way to provide great customer service.) New Partners would buy a collection of our best-selling items at a discount, which meant they had a few lovely items for display with the option to purchase additional items at a discounted price for themselves.

As we grew, I assumed more of a leadership role within Trades of Hope, eventually embracing the title of CEO. This gave me the flexibility and opportunity to make each day look and feel different—a personal value for me. Some days were for meetings or countless conversations with our US Partners, and other days I appreciated an excuse to pack boxes in the distribution center. A girl can only sit on a laptop for so long, no matter what kind of company title she carries! The relief I felt working in the warehouse after long hours on the phone or my laptop gave me flashbacks to when I was a little girl, bored and restless out of my mind, sitting quietly in a church pew at St. Agnes' (second row on the left, just in case you church girls were wondering!). Then, I became an altar girl in our parish as a young teen. (I told you the priest was more "progressive"—hence his idea for girls to participate in a role normally reserved for boys.) Sitting still in a pew for so long was difficult, and I had a hard time paying attention in church. But I loved having a job during Mass, which made it so much easier to absorb what was being taught. As a young girl, and now as a grown woman, an active body meant an engaged mind for me.

Later on, I would discover I had ADD, now often referred to as "inattentive ADHD."[23] (Recently, I've learned that 3 out of 10 people who have dyslexia also have ADHD.[24]) But I went undiagnosed for a long time because I wasn't hyperactive or as impulsive as some individuals with classic ADHD symptoms. I just struggled to pay attention, remember things, and not get so easily distracted. It wasn't until my friend Cindy gave a talk at our annual Direct Sales Association conference a few years ago that I realized I had a bit of a problem. Cindy was someone I knew and admired, but as she stood up front, I totally blanked on her name. I couldn't remember it for the life of me until I looked down at my schedule for the day, where her name was printed in bold. I drove straight home from the conference and made an appointment with my doctor, convinced I had the start of dementia. I was in his office a few days later to explain. After sharing my symptoms through some tears, he kindly leaned over and softly said,

"Gretchen, you do not have dementia. You have a problem with work concentration. Otherwise known as ADD, my friend."

Phew! What a relief.

I learned how to lead with ADD and then put some new practices into place. One of those practices was understanding the connection between an active body and an engaged brain. That's why I didn't mind packing products in the storage units. It was where I did some of my best thinking, planning, and collaborating with the rest of the team.

Back to little Gretchen as an altar girl for a brief moment. I never ever doubted there was a God who loved me and a family who wanted the best for me. And I think those beliefs were what gave me such a strong sense of security in childhood and a strong sense of purpose in the world. It was my childhood faith that shaped the trajectory of my life. I always knew the love of Jesus and his words (translated by his followers) about caring for others, especially widows and orphans.[25] So it wasn't a crazy idea that God would "call us" or "ask" me to do something to help people in need. From day one, I felt called to the work of caring for others—to fill a gap so others could thrive.

And know this, it's okay if that language of "calling" doesn't work for you.

Either way, I hope there are pieces of my purpose and passion that resonate with you and encourage you to do the very thing you feel called or compelled to do.

That's why I'm sharing the rest of my story here, with you.

Chapter Seven

TESTING YOUR THEORIES

One Thousand Ways

WHEN I WAS A LITTLE GIRL, the best thing about daycare was the Barbie selection. And the worst part for my active body and curious imagination was the afternoon nap. (Naps were torture!) I loved dressing those Barbie dolls and changing their clothes according to their daily activities, which I made up on my own. This is probably where I started caring so much about fashion. And my mother was (and still is) a fashionable lady. She always made sure I had cute clothes to wear. I still remember the pink plastic box with a white bow on top I had as a little girl, full of my grandma's costume jewelry. I loved all of the dress-up jewelry, costumes, and pomp and circumstance that came with piano lessons, dance recitals, musical theater, pom-pom squad, high school formals, and even dressing up for church.

When I think about how hard my mom worked and yet still prioritized all of these extra things for me (in addition to paying for weekly tutoring), it amazes me. I really admire and appreciate all of her sacrifices as I look back on those formative years. In elementary school, I noticed how some moms stayed home with their kids and volunteered at school. But I never wished my mom was anyone but herself. I hope my children say the same one day—that they admire and appreciate the way I showed up in life. I also realize just how lucky my brother and I were to have such a "normal" life, even after my parents divorced. The confidence I held from such a secure childhood, including great friendships, carried me throughout my own life circumstances and the leadership of two organizations.

This kind of confidence is what helped us grow Trades of Hope to 12 million dollars in sales by 2017. But it didn't happen overnight. Those first few years were quite the uphill climb. It was so much fun but a ton of work. With Trades of Hope, I found an effective solution for alleviating poverty, but I had to learn more about managing a company and growing a business. Running a nonprofit in Haiti with a small staff and a lot of volunteers was way different than running a for-profit business in the US. Thanks to Google, a few great mentors, and a lot of business books, I learned how to manage employees: how to hire, fire, and have hard conversations that my Midwestern self was not particularly good at when we first started. We also had to learn about the customs and cultures of more than one country if we wanted to do business in a way that aligned with our values. Honesty, integrity, and transparency were always at the forefront of every partnership, but these words held different meanings in various cultures.

THE FAIR-TRADE CHOICE

Right from the start, our philosophy was to work directly with Artisan Partners. Our soft launch with wholesale products made by Artisans for Ten Thousand Villages told us exactly what we needed to know: *there was a market in the US for fair-trade fashion with mission-minded women.* And there were established Artisan groups all over the world looking for new wholesale partners like us—partners willing to agree to the Fair Trade Federation's (FTF) *Federation Principles.*[26] We were willing to commit to and believe in all ten FTF principles, but the ones we primarily share with our customers and Partners today are:

The Fair Trade Federation's (FTF) *Fair-Trade Principles*

- Pay Promptly & Fairly
- Support Safe & Empowering Work Conditions
- Respect Cultural, Racial, & Ethnic Identity
- Build Capacity Through Long-Term Relationships

More detailed information is available at www.fairtradefederation.org

This is what it meant to consider our standards and products "fair-trade." And this is what it meant to be Trades of Hope.

In my mind, fair-trade practices were an example of what separated charity work from development work. There's a space and a need for charity when it comes to disaster aid and crisis relief. However, from my perspective, development is the path to long-term solutions and sustainable outcomes. Charity is what helps communities *survive*, but development is what helps communities *thrive*.

Part of that commitment to supporting sustainable development for thriving communities meant that we worked with Artisan Partners who were creating and crafting based on their local, indigenous, or traditional trade. In Haiti, there were Artisan groups making artwork out of steel drums and jewelry out of rolled cardboard from leftover cereal boxes. In the Dominican Republic, Artisans were stringing beaded bracelets made of a rare genuine Larimar stone that can only be found in its native volcanic regions. In Guatemala, women were making jewelry out of sterling silver and leather bags handcrafted with upcycled Mayan Huipil. Huipil is a beautiful handwoven material woven on a loom. The traditional patterns are worn on blouses by women in Guatemala to signify which region they call home. Each piece was one of a kind, featuring Huipil colors, patterns, and motifs unique to each Artisan's village. In East Asia, Artisans were crafting resin jewelry mixed with semi-precious stones and dried flowers. In India, women were hand-stitching Kantha fabric and using block printing skills taught to them by their mothers and grandmothers. And the list goes on.

ARTISAN PARTNERS

My original idea of micro-financing was more complicated than my initial glance. I realized later, even after we started Trades of Hope, how much on-the-ground training, education, and guidance is needed to create a successful micro-financing program. However, purchasing from Artisan Partners still created opportunities for women in the most desperate, poverty-stricken places around the world and in the US. It's been inspiring to see women who were living in survival mode step into something new, empowering, and bold.

Some of these Artisan groups have been established for 50-plus years. They were the outgrowth of the work of Methodist missionary women who saw the beautiful traditional beadwork, baskets, stitching, jewelry, fashion, and home accessories created in indigenous communities where women were often relegated to lives of poverty. So these missionary women started gathering women in groups as they practiced their traditional craft or skill. And then they established export routes to Australia, England, the Netherlands, and other parts of Europe where there was already an awareness of and a market for fair-trade goods. It took us a while longer to understand the benefit of fair trade in the US. Our markets are driven more by a consumer mindset, meaning we want more for less. And fair trade is often "less for more"—fewer options or inventory with more craftsmanship and more value.

The Artisan group model worked well because it brought women together in their communities to work on things many of them had already been doing on their own. There were also instances where the fair-trade products made by these Artisan groups required a new skill based on market demands in other areas of the world. In these cases, the missionary women provided translated resources or patterns the women needed to learn how to make a new product. Once these women started supporting themselves, the Artisan groups were no longer just a means of survival, they were a breath of fresh air—a chance for women to come together in community, share stories and songs, and make old things new. And the salaries they made from the goods they sold provided the necessary resources to rise above poverty.

After a few months of selling fair-trade goods sourced wholesale by Ten Thousand Villages and the Haitian women working with my friend Shelley, we started networking with more people to work directly with other Artisan Partner groups. This didn't mean we were their only partner—many Artisan groups work with more than one wholesale partner. It meant we found partnerships in places where we wanted to invest deep roots and help women alleviate poverty in their lives and find safety from the dangers of human trafficking. One by one, we established relationships with Artisan Partner groups around the world. And one by one, their handmade, fashionable goods were sold by our sales consultants to women in the US.

With ongoing Artisan partnerships and unique handcrafted products readily available for purchase, the possibilities were endless. And that was exciting for us! It was also the unlimited variety and constant opportunity for growth at every angle that kept things interesting for me in the work we were doing. I loved the products and fashion we found. I loved our partnerships with these Artisan groups. And I loved that this work meant job creation and sustainable change for women and their families all over the globe. My friend Milan says,

"When women gather, magic happens."

Our Artisan Partner groups were living proof of that magic!

BACK TO MY *WHY*

The business was coming together in such beautiful ways, and I was lucky enough to be living out my *why*—the reason why I started Trades of Hope. But I wasn't naive to the stories of mission drift— the idea that companies would slowly drift away from the original mission and vision of why they got started in the first place. For this reason, our team talks a lot about the women we are working with and putting people above profits. I also learned a helpful tool for digging deep from one of our Partners at a leader's retreat one year. It was the "Seven-Levels Deep Exercise"[27] (everyone from the Midwest thought I was about to describe a seven-layer salad, didn't you?!). Here's how this exercise works, and I'm sharing this because I think it could be helpful for you, too:

7-Layer *WHY* Exercise:

- Ask yourself *why* you're doing what you're doing
- Write down your answer
- In response to your answer, ask yourself *"why?"* again
- Do this seven times until you get to your last *why* answer. Usually, this is your most essential reason *why*—the reason that drives everything you do!

Exercise attributed to and adapted from multiple sources

I was thankful that by the time I got down to my own essential *why* on the seventh time, it was still the same mission I was living that day:

To alleviate poverty for women and keep children with their mothers.

And I lived this out at Trades of Hope with my answer to the first why question:

To create job opportunities for women so they could make their own choices and grow.

First came the job opportunities, then came the alleviation of poverty so mothers could keep their children. This was my reason *why*!

For Elisabeth, her *why* as part of Trades of Hope blossomed into empowering women using fair-trade fashion as a force for good. This would eventually become our trademarked mission: Fashion as a *Force for Good.*™ But the full picture of Elisabeth's *why* is to help women experience gender equality in socially oppressive communities through financial independence. Some people may think Elisabeth grew into this business because I was her mother and she was doing this with me. Yes, we were in this business *together*, but she was her own person with her own strengths and ideas. (And she still is today!) Elisabeth was just as much a business partner as she was my daughter.

Elisabeth spending the day with Artisan Partners in India

She spent her childhood traveling to Haiti and witnessing some of the same experiences I did. She held babies while they cried and said goodbye to their birth moms or their adoptive moms who were visiting and had to leave them behind and go back to the US to wait out the adoption process. She helped give vaccines to women at the medical clinic alongside my sister Jen. She had her own personal ties to Haiti and her own reasons for wanting to create job opportunities and help women up and out of poverty.

I can still picture Elisabeth as a teenager, calculating commissions and writing checks to our sales field from her bedroom desk on Saturday mornings. Throughout her undergraduate years at college, she helped with our administrative tasks, our partnerships, and our product development. She took photos and created graphics for our e-newsletter and social media presence. Elisabeth eventually became our Chief Brand Officer. My passion was alleviating poverty through job opportunities for women and their children, and her passion was empowering women to rise out of oppressive cultures to experience equality and opportunity through financial independence. (Yes, she is much more eloquent than I am.) Our passions went hand in hand with helping women in Artisan Partner groups and raising awareness about gender inequalities and ethical fashion.

Artisan Partner communities were our way of establishing what we referred to as *dignified partnerships.* Maintaining dignity was, and will always be, a top priority for us. I knew there was a slippery slope between development ideas and charity services, and I wanted to make sure every partnership was dignified by the guardrails of development rather than characterized by the handouts of charity. I think many of us forget when we are out shopping or making decisions on what we buy that *who makes it matters!* Meaning, every woman who handcrafts and creates the accessories we sell matters to us. This would always be true as long as we were mindful of our mission. We could sell anything as long as we recognized the dignity and contribution of the woman behind the products. When women have dignified, healthy experiences at work, they can be the heroes of their own stories and teach their children how to do and be the same.

We also worked with a few men connected to our Artisan Partner groups. For example, we met educated men in India who genuinely cared about the plight of women living in poverty around them. To these men, the women near them were their fellow sisters. They knew about fair trade from their own business ventures or educational travel to other parts of the world. As a result, several of these men developed Artisan Partner group models that worked well in their local communities. Eventually, one of these men would join the staff at Trades of Hope. Lucas Caldeira used to be the leader of one of the largest fair-trade organizations in India, a member of the World Fair Trade Federation board, and now, he is a liaison with Trades of Hope. He and his wife, Diana, visit our Artisan Partner groups in India and throughout the rest of Asia and Africa to establish deep connections, help ensure fair-trade principles are followed, and build business partnerships. Lucas and Diana are lovely human beings! His wisdom and cultural understanding have been a huge asset to our team.

THE DIRECT SALES MODEL

Our relationships with our Artisan Partner groups wouldn't be successful without the support of our sales consultants in the US. These women are the backbone of our business and why more women worldwide are experiencing full and vibrant lives beyond poverty. This is what we call the *Sisterhood* of Trades of Hope.

When we first started adding consultants to our team, we called them Compassionate Entrepreneurs. That's literally what they were—compassionate women who were entrepreneurs and CEOs of their own small Trades of Hope businesses. As it turns out, the term Compassionate Entrepreneurs caused confusion because it wasn't clear or concise, so we switched to calling our sales consultants *Partners*. I liked this term much more as it leaned into my desire to create dignified partnerships with other women. Now we had Artisan Partners from our Artisan communities around the globe and Partners who were the consultants selling our exclusive line of ethically-made accessories in the US. This is the full circle of what we refer to as dignified partnerships.

In the early years of our business, the Direct Sales Association (DSA) was a powerhouse of businesses, leaders, products, and goods. Mary Kay was one of the pioneers of the industry, but other companies, many of them led by female CEOs, made their way into mainstream markets and online retail. In addition to Mary Kay, there was Pampered Chef, Thirty-One Gifts, Tastefully Simple, Jordan Essentials, SeneGence, Scentsy, Vantel Pearls, and the list goes on! Some of these companies, such as Avon and Tupperware, have been empowering women since the 1940s as the CEOs of their own small businesses. And some have already gone past the $100 million dollar mark in revenue, with a select few soaring towards one billion—all through home-party style sales. Incredible!

However, none of these direct sales companies were fair-trade organizations. This meant the Direct Sales Association conferences were a fun treat but not always directly applicable. The greatest value of our DSA membership has been the women business owners who have become our mentors and some of my closest friends. I had an instant community with these peers and lots of opportunities to learn from what worked and didn't work well in their companies. Most of them have been transparent about their successes, their mistakes, and the lessons they learned along the way. In fact, I remember one CEO-peer whom I really admired told me, "The more employees you have, the less productive everyone will be." Her wisdom made me more comfortable with staying relatively small at our home office compared to some other companies. I thought my Direct Sales CEO peers would prove to be quite competitive, but instead, they were warm and kind. And smart, *so very smart!* I have learned, grown, laughed, cried, and explored the world alongside some of these amazing women. Direct sales has not only been a whole lot of fun for me, but much more importantly, it has been a way to make an unlimited impact involving thousands of women around the world.

From my perspective, there was a common spirit shared with my DSA peers. We all built small businesses into something successful with grit, purpose, determination, Google searches, and duct tape. What I mean is that I believe everything is searchable, figure-out-able, and there's nothing that won't "stick" when it's made out of perseverance and passion. I would never have considered the direct sales model an option had it not been for Holly. And I'm so grateful this was the path we collectively chose.

Direct sales highlighted the power of women helping other women in ways that selling fair-trade goods through the traditional retail model of brick-and-mortar stores didn't. Women selling fair-trade fashion on behalf of thousands of Artisan Partners and sisters around the globe was really special and very empowering. It created an "abundance mindset" for our Partners in the US to make a profit in their own pockets, knowing their profits created opportunities for other women, rather than taking profits away from them. This was what we referred to as the "rising tide" of our sisterhood, thanks to ethical fashion. Because of the direct sales model—including the opportunity to make direct purchases online—when one of us rises with a successful tide of sales, we all have the opportunity to rise.

The direct sales model keeps our Artisan Partners as our first priority. And every US Partner has understood this priority from the start of their business with us. Truth is, most of our Partners live in areas where they could find other jobs if they no longer wanted, or needed, to be part of our Trades of Hope team. But our Artisan Partners don't have that same luxury. These groups depend on wholesale orders from businesses like ours. That's why all of our decisions regarding our Partners are made in light of how those decisions affect our Artisan Partners. My hope is that we never have to move away from the direct sales, home-party business plan as a way to prioritize Artisan Partners. It's the best way to share stories, build community, and empower other women all over the US and the rest of the world.

OUR US PARTNERS

When we started adding sales consultants in 2011, these Partners were mostly Midwestern, mission-minded women who knew us personally and Floridians from our community in Palm Coast. They were our friends, family members, and the women who followed our journey with Three Angels, and now Trades of Hope, from afar—usually connected to us through someone else in our community. They were moms and caregivers—biological moms, foster moms, adoptive moms—and women from all walks of life who had proximity to foster care resources and adoptive family support. Many of these women were faith-filled, even though they would all explain what that meant in different ways. Some of them had full-time jobs, and others had a second part-time gig besides their work with Trades of Hope. Some were retired professionals in other industries. A lot of these women were stay-at-home moms looking to provide for their families in additional ways. And the same is true today.

Our Partners are taking care of their family and friends, juggling a million things, working on their confidence, driven by their love for others and their faith in God, and excited about the opportunity to earn extra income—knowing they're also helping their global sisters do the same. They get to make a difference and help alleviate poverty by selling fair-trade fashion in their hometown on their own time. An appealing mission for these busy women. While other direct sales companies were offering big commission checks, prizes, and incentive trips, we were working hard to encourage our Partners to accept the commission profits they made from the products they sold. I remember one Partner who called us on the phone steaming mad after she received a commission check in the mail a few days after her first party.

"I thought all of the money went to Artisan Partners!" she said, nearly shouting through the phone.

It took a few attempts to explain how our Artisan Partners had already been paid for the products we received from them—the very same products she sold a few nights earlier. And how our business model worked both ways. Products were fairly purchased and fairly priced, so both our Partners and our Artisan Partners made a fair wage. It wasn't a preference; it was a fair-trade standard. And that was my standard, too.

Then I heard myself say, "If you want to give it all away, that's your prerogative!" (I'm all about women having choices.) That was it. She continued to sell Trades of Hope products for many years to come, encouraged by the impact she knew she was making around the world and enjoying her commissions.

Our goal was to be long-term and sustainable with each group we worked with, including our Partners. We knew that if the women selling the products were earning an income too, then they would stick with it longer. Of course, they would! I would, too, if I were in their position. *Wouldn't you?* Providing a profit for the women selling our products was how we grew and placed even more orders in the years to come. But it also made me mindful of making sure we placed *consistent* monthly orders with our Artisan Partners—orders they could rely on rather than the big "flash in the pan" orders. This was how we measured our growth and success as the Artisan's business partner. *Were we doing more than just one order with each group? If not, what needed to happen so we could provide more consistent orders for more sustainable business partnerships?* For this reason, we gather our Partners and Artisan Partners on a group video call together once a month. This is a chance for Partners to hear the stories of our Artisan Partners and learn more about the products and pieces we sell. I love these calls because I want our Partners to understand that the work of Trades of Hope isn't about "saving" anyone—it's about giving women opportunities to grow into whatever or whomever they were meant to be when they're no longer confined by poverty. We also make these monthly calls a priority because we also believe our Artisans should be using their voices and sharing their stories in their own words.

If you've ever been part of a direct sales company, you're probably curious about our structure and incentives. According to other direct sales businesses, we honored our Partners by providing a similar growth track. Partners could earn their way from being an entry-level Partner, through many tiers, to National Executive Director. Each tier had sales-performance measures and values-alignment markers. Partner earnings were (and still are) based on sales, not recruitment of others (earnings based on simply recruiting others is known as a "pyramid scheme"—this is illegal). Trades of Hope Partners earn income based on the commission of their own sales and a percentage of commissions based on the sales of the rest of their team. Some Partners have actually replaced the income they were earning in other full-time jobs, now having much more flexibility and purpose. This is rare, but I know many others are thrilled to earn a few extra hundred dollars each month for their families. Building a direct sales business requires a lot of time, energy, and self-discipline. But our Partners often tell me how much it's been worth it. They tell me how earning money has made them feel like they can take care of their families and have choices about how they spend and invest their money, too. And to all of them, that feels very good.

Some Partners have even shared just how meaningful it has been to support their husbands in ways their husbands have been supporting them for years. One of our Partners said that for so long, her husband had been working hard and putting his family's needs above his own. So she took some of the commission money she saved from her home parties over the years and, one Christmas, handed her husband a beautiful box with $10,000 in it. There was one stipulation: he had to spend the money on something he needed or wanted *for himself*, or he could save it, but it had to be his choice. Another Partner ordered a backyard shed for her husband and had it delivered as a surprise. Many Partners have paid for their family's Christmas gifts with their earnings or taken their families on special trips. Others have covered annual grocery expenses and dance classes for their little ones. We've heard countless stories like these over the years.

Earning a livable wage for our Partners and our Artisan Partners brings everyone so much JOY! *(To make sure I am keeping the Federal Trade Commission happy, I would like to add this little disclaimer: The majority of our consultants earn a modest supplemental income. Stories shared represent less than 1% of income earners in any direct sales company. You're welcome, FTC.)*

Direct sales, especially fair-trade direct sales companies, are not a "get rich quick" kind of thing. It's too bad that people outside the industry have viewed direct sales this way for a long time. For us, it was simply the most effective way to create change and allow so many other women to be a part of it. I know from experience that it takes a few years of consistent home parties to build the business I had imagined. It's the women who have a long-term vision, a heart for the mission, and tenacity who are successful at building their own Trades of Hope small businesses. Above all else, a direct sales model in a fair-trade world means we can treat our people well *and* make sustainable profits. It doesn't always have to be "people over profits." It can be both. This is what I mean by having an "abundance" mindset.

What started as one thousand ways to test Artisan partnerships and theories about fair-trade product development turned out to be a successful direct sales business in just a few short years. But a growing bottom line wasn't our only metric of success. We knew we were becoming a success when we saw women from our Artisan Partner groups and our team of sales consultant Partners go from surviving to thriving, all because of each other.

That's when I knew this would all be worth it.

Chapter Eight

IMAGINING POSSIBILITIES

Think Outside the Box

AS A LITTLE KID, I thought I could do anything and be anything when I grew up. But as a 25-year-old young mom, the dream of doing something big and important beyond the walls of our California home felt elusive. And my track record was enough to prove this point before I even tried. I got pregnant, dropped out of college, ran off to Europe with Frits, eventually got married, and settled down. Although for Frits and I, "settling down" meant moving to the most viable consulting job opportunities for him. Our life together was secure, and yet we were anything but "normal." Because of so many moves, Elisabeth and Harrison, our older two, never really had the chance to find childhood friends like I had. And that's okay. It's just different from what I expected. What I expected was a life a lot like mine, growing up in the same home with grandparents who lived next door and sixth-grade friends who stayed together throughout the years and life's ups and downs.

I guess it's true that some of us live the opposite of what we've always known. In spite of moving around so much when our kids were little, we still loved our lives and our home—wherever that was in the moment. But I also had things my mom never had, including the opportunity to stay home with my young children and a super supportive husband. Frits supported my decision to be home with our kids, my decision to open a nonprofit in Haiti, and my decision to start Trades of Hope. I am forever grateful for his thoughtful, loving encouragement.

In fact, I naively thought I always had everyone's support.

I'll never forget the time I was having lunch with my mom, and she said, "You know, someone asked me at lunch the other day if I ever thought Gretchen would run a big, successful business, and I said 'No!' I mean, you never even finished college!" She meant it as a passing compliment while we were sitting together in the restaurant. But, if I'm being honest, it took part of me a few months to recover from the hurt I felt after that comment. For one thing, not finishing my degree was a point of insecurity for me for a long time. And for forty-plus years, I lived under the illusion my mom believed I could be anything I wanted to be and do anything I put my mind to. The realization that there were times when she doubted what I could actually do, namely run a successful business like Trades of Hope, rocked my world a little bit. But I got over it and moved on. (Mom, don't be mad that I'm telling this story. Please, keep reading.) When I put myself in her shoes, I realized she never envisioned running a multi-million dollar business herself, let alone one of her children doing so. (My brother Michael has a very successful crop-dusting aviation business, too. Two wins for mom!)

Another time we were visiting my mom at her house. I was catching up on a few work things one afternoon when I looked up from my computer and casually mentioned to Frits that we were at $27,000 in sales so far. My mom looked up and asked,

"For the year?"

And I said,

"No, Mom. For today."

She looked at me with disbelief and surprise.

I don't think anyone outside of our innermost circles understood for a long time just how big Trades of Hope had grown. But I didn't help that perception either. It took me a full eighteen months to ask one of my family members to host a Trades of Hope home party. So I couldn't take their questions (or possible doubts) personally. I also didn't leave much room for opinions from friends and family because sometimes the people closest to us are the hardest to convince of our passion and our plans. In the beginning, not many people outside of my immediate family and our co-founders understood the vision, especially with a direct sales model, and I didn't want any negative feedback. So, I just didn't ask.

I don't regret the beautiful trajectory of my life, even though some people would probably say I did it all backward, namely the baby before the marriage. I love the life Frits and I have built together. And yet, there were also times as a young mom when I started to feel as though I was losing myself. Age twenty-five was one of those times. I didn't have a clue what I could contribute to the world at that point, and that was unnerving for me. I wasn't used to feeling insignificant. While Frits traveled and created a very successful career for himself, I dropped the kids off at preschool and roamed the aisles of Target. And then felt guilty for not being full of gratitude. I felt this way until my passion and my dreams became more clear. Outside of our little family, I found my dream with the start of Three Angels, then another dream when we brought Mia home, and yet another when it came time to launch Trades of Hope. Pursuing those dreams with the support of the people who loved me most allowed me to imagine all of the possibilities and find work I felt passionate about.

SPENDING POWER

Now, my dream is for women in developing countries to have job opportunities so they can care for their families and for women in the US to recognize the power of every dollar we spend. When we spend our money in fair and ethical ways, we lift the economic tide in equitable ways for all. Spending our money in fair and ethical ways means:

1. Making sure the products we purchase acknowledge the person(s) who made the product, how they were treated, and how they were paid.

AND

2. Having a third-party stamp of approval that they operate at a fair, dignified standard.

When you doubt whether or not the piece you're about to purchase is made in fair and ethical ways, the Fair Trade Federation and Fair Trade Certification symbols are always stamps of confidence and approval.

If I see this mark, then I don't have to ask where, how, and by whom the product was made. I've been known to email and message companies to ask those questions if it's not obvious on the packaging or the website. Usually, I write: *"How do you ensure that the people making your products have safe working conditions and earn living*

154

wages?" If they don't respond, then nine times out of ten, I move on to find a similar product by a more socially conscious provider.

I'm also the first to admit that I love to spend a day shopping with my sisters at TJ Maxx or pick up something cute without checking to see where and how it's made. It's my personal goal to continue purchasing more ethically-made products and fewer unethically (possibly) made products each year. For me, this also means buying less . . . and I'm becoming okay with that. Ethical spending isn't always about a new set of shopping "rules" or purchasing fair-trade with every single thing you buy. It's about *recognizing the power of every dollar you spend.*

ETHICAL FASHION

We should also expect that any brand of substance is asking these crucial questions about how their product manufacturers are being treated and getting paid. It is estimated that only 2% of the fashion industry's workers earn a living wage.[28] Being treated fairly and earning a living wage are basic human rights. We're not saying companies should cover everyone's college tuition or send their employees to the Moon. Some fashion brands such as Eileen Fisher, Burberry, and Chloe are showing the high-end designer world that it's possible to be successful and pay living wages to their workers. I am still baffled by how many brands don't talk about who makes their products and have no response when I inquire. Every time I grow tired of spending time emailing a retailer to see if the item I'm purchasing is made ethically according to fair-trade standards, I think of these powerful words I read by Malala Yousafzai:

"When the world is silent, even one voice becomes powerful."

And I remind myself that in that moment, searching for contact information to write a quick email, I may be the "one voice" right now. Truth is, we all have the opportunity to be that "one voice" at any given moment in any given opportunity.

We didn't start Trades of Hope to disrupt the fashion industry. And that's still not our core mission today. However, while pursuing our vision of women leading their families out of poverty through job creation, we learned the power of our dollars. Safe workplaces and fair wages are what we would want for ourselves and our children's future. So why not demand it for our sisters, too? For us, this means advocating for safe workplaces and fair wages for the men and women who make our clothing, jewelry, accessories, and home goods. This is the work and the vision that gets me out of bed every morning.

THE TIME IT TAKES TO BUILD

Looking back over our timeline, I'm still amazed at the work we accomplished in the first twelve years at Trades of Hope. I share our full timeline in the appendix at the back of the book to encourage you with whatever dream you're building. It takes time to make things happen. And yet hindsight will show you just how fast the process really goes. The same was true for us.

Leading this business has allowed me (and, at times, even *forced* me) to learn, grow, and be challenged. I've learned how to navigate really hard conversations and successfully have a self-motivated, self-starter team. We are a team of quick learners, problem solvers, and solution seekers—and *this* is the kind of team I can manage well. The truth is, I'm not great at managing people who need a lot of time and attention, in other words, *a lot of hand-holding*. But the people on our team are amazing at developing others, a quality that makes them skilled with entry-level employees who need more connection and time. I've gone from feeling insecure as a leader to accepting my leadership style and feeling proud of myself when I'm leading well.

As I write this, we have a leadership team that includes two executives, one honorary executive (Frits), and four full-time managing professionals. We had a third executive whom we loved and adored as our COO, but Jeremy worked his way out of his role and decided it was time to move on. This was a hard decision for him and a hard release for me. He was the backbone of our operations, processes, procedures, and the key to developing our team in so many ways. Then he showed us that the people he had been developing for years were ready to rise into leadership positions. They were more than capable and equipped to step up when he decided to step out (in an incredibly honorable way). Now, we are a company *by* women, *for* women, *led* by women, with an all-female leadership team in the home office. These women have imagined all of the possibilities with me and have been willing to think outside the box, even when it came to their roles—many of which have morphed and changed over time. Now, it is my great pleasure to introduce you to our all-female management team:

- **Product Design & Development | Julie**

Along with Elisabeth, Julie is our eyes and ears for fashion trends and new creative ideas. She came to us right out of college with a degree in Fibers and Textiles and a desire to design with impact and do good in the world. She works with every Artisan Partner group on new products for the upcoming season. She not only designs beautiful jewelry and handbags with the Artisans, but she is also a dream to work with every day.

· Accounts Payable & Distribution | Melissa

Melissa is one of the longest-standing members of our team, developing decade-long relationships with all of us and our Artisan Partners. She works with her team to place orders with the Artisans, following those orders until they reach us in Florida. She also ensures there is quality control and that inventory is managed, bills are paid, and all orders are shipped to you as the customer. Logistics and numbers are her thing!

· Human Resources & Events | Michelle

Michelle served with me at Three Angels when we were still running the orphanage. She's also an adoptive mom. Michelle is great at the art of gathering people and making everyone feel seen and celebrated. She is our people-person, handling things from human resource tasks to team building days and INSPIRE. We'd be lost without her on the team. (We'd certainly be way less fun.)

· Customer Care & Partner Development | Stacie

Stacie oversees Partner training and customer service. She's the woman who blows me away each day. She is somehow incredibly sweet but very strong at the same time. She will jump in to learn whatever is needed and is always determined to figure things out. Stacie joined Trades of Hope in an entry-level position and has worked her way up to be an industry professional and team MVP.

· Brand Communications & Marketing | Elisabeth

Elisabeth is a co-founder and my oldest daughter. She oversees everything branding, communications strategy, marketing, visual storytelling, sales training, and customer experience. She is passionate about speaking unapologetic confidence into women—the women on our home team, our Artisans, and our Partners. She's also developed a career coaching practice for women (when she isn't also coaching women inside of our business). Elisabeth has a lot of say about global justice for women and ethical fashion, which we'll share in chapter 10 (except for the stuff she'll share in her own book someday!).

- **Leadership & Strategy | Me**

While I love to have fun, I am very serious about my role as co-founder and CEO. I cast vision, create strategy, and allocate resources, but also still make day-to-day decisions. I love coming up with new ideas and creating new opportunities within Trades of Hope, while ensuring our mission always remains the focus of everything we do as a team.

All of these women, including myself, have grown into our roles as respected professionals in the direct sales and fair-trade industries. And Frits continues to be super supportive of me, Elisabeth, and everyone on our team. He loves our mission, our partnerships, and our company presence. In fact, there are weeks when Frits puts as much time into the business as I do! But he's not the only guy on our team. As I mentioned earlier, Lucas works from India with our Artisan Partner groups in that region as a liaison helping to source and develop new products and, from time to time, new groups. He brings a ton of experience as a former leader in the fair-trade industry in his corner of the world. We also have valued employees on our Manager's teams. Some of whom have been with us since the very beginning.

What a team! I'm so honored and blessed to work alongside this amazing group of people (customer care team, writers, administrators, technical support, graphic designers, and distribution team) who also value being part of the mission to help mothers keep their children and alleviate human trafficking. I enjoy going into the office to work with these people every day.

OUTSIDE THE BOX

Because we address things like poverty and human trafficking in a beautiful yet thoughtful way with fashion and accessories, it was (and still is) hard for people to grasp the impact at times. I remember traveling in a taxi in Japan with an older woman who was an artist. We were both on a sightseeing trip with author John Shors. He wrote a book about Cambodia and Southeast Asia called *Temple of a Thousand Faces*. A few years later, he offered a trip for readers to explore the places he wrote about in the book.

I was in the back of a taxi with Frits on one side of me and an older woman on the other. She asked me what I did, so I told her about Trades of Hope. She listened for a few minutes and then leaned in, patted my hand, and said,

"Oh, you have such a beautiful little business!"

I know she was being kind, but I wondered at that moment if people would say the same thing to Frits when he explained his consulting business. *Oh, Frits, you have such a beautiful little business!* Could you imagine? But our "beautiful little business" would grow to have an impact in more ways than Elisabeth, Frits, or I could have imagined. And the best part? We were honest, authentic, and true to our mission and vision every step of the way. I think it was hard for people to wrap their minds around our work because it was "outside the box" of what they knew about having and growing a business versus a typical charity. A business can put people first *and* help people thrive as long as the mission is never forgotten.

In 2019, Elisabeth wrote a draft of our manifesto based on conversations we were having. I absolutely loved it. According to Merriam-Webster, a manifesto is *a written statement declaring publicly the intentions, motives, or views of its issuer.*[29] Our manifesto still stirs emotion in me as I read it years later.

Our Manifesto:

Each style is the physical expression of a woman's transformation.

Women around the world and their strength are our muse.

We have a vision of the world where women—from nation to nation—live unapologetically joyful lives.

We are women who know what we want and create the opportunity to reach it.

We believe that success is not a lofty goal reserved for a few. It's found in every woman who rises each day to show up as her beautifully imperfect self.

We make no apologies for the success, boldness, and influence we work to create for women near and far.

From Artisan to Partner, our income gives us confidence, pride, and peace of mind.

Because of our work, we radiate as our true selves. And we collectively rise to illuminate a more hopeful world.

We are ONE WORLD. WOMEN. RISING. TOGETHER.

A Trades of Hope manifesto was important because the worlds of fair trade, fashion, and sustainable development in developing countries were far and wide. We needed both an anchor and a compass if we wanted to find our footing as we moved back and forth between those worlds. It became a helpful guide as we navigated business rhythms such as strategic planning, partnerships, product development, sales and marketing, brand alignment, and bringing on new Partners who sold our products and accessories. And it served as inspiration and accountability for how we showed up with our Artisan Partners, our US Partners, our fair-trade and retail colleagues, and our direct sales peers.

If you were to write your own manifesto about how you wished to show up in the world, *what would it look or sound like for you? Want to give it a try?* If so, take a few moments to think through the intentions, motives, and aspirations you wish to "publicly declare" about the way you live your life or operate your business. Then write down a draft of those thoughts here. It's always helpful to have an anchor, a compass, and a guide no matter what stage, age, or season you find yourself in, even if it's for your eyes only. I promise you will thank me later. Ask yourself questions like:

> *What do you want to see change/happen in the world?*
> *What are your strongest beliefs? (What do you know to be true?)*
> *What actions would you be doing that you aren't doing today?*
> *How do you want to treat yourself?*
> *How do you want to treat others?*
> *What do you want to accomplish within your life or your business?*
> *If you were already successful in accomplishing your vision, how would you show up and carry yourself every day?*

Now, rewrite your answers to those questions using positive, uplifting, bold language in the present tense. Feel free to use our manifesto as your guide. I hope you create something helpful *and* beautiful. It should give you chills when you read it!

Your Manifesto:

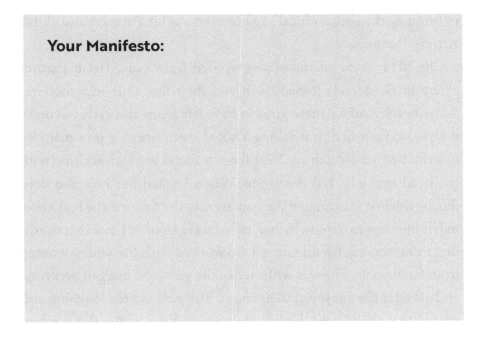

INSPIRE

One of the ways we've lived out our manifesto, even before it became our "official" manifesto, is to gather the women in our Trades of Hope sisterhood in person at least once a year. In 2014, we started hosting annual conferences held in Florida that we now called *INSPIRE*. These conferences are both a trend and a tradition. An annual gathering is also our best chance to celebrate the previous year's global impact, provide an exciting reveal of the upcoming sales season, and vision cast for the new year. Most importantly, it's a time to connect with everyone as we live out our culture of valuing and celebrating each other. My favorite part about INSPIRE isn't just being together with our Partners (though I do love this more than I could have ever imagined!), it is including our Artisan Partners in the experience, too. We have made specific invitations with all expenses covered to bring various Artisans from different countries over the years. It's our way of bridging the geographical gap between our US Partners and global Artisan Partners.

In 2015, some of the young women from our Artisan Partner group in Guatemala joined us. It was their first time in a modern, 4-star hotel. And for these girls, in their late teens and early twenties, it was also their first time taking a hot shower, sleeping on a mattress in a real bed, and watching TV. I'll never forget my conversation with the head nun who led the group. When I asked her how she slept during the first morning of the conference, she told me she had never in her life slept in a room by herself. *And she loved it!* Later that morning, I ran into my friend Clare, who worked with the young women from Guatemala. She was with two of the girls, so I hugged everyone and asked if they enjoyed their room. The girls started laughing and shared that they loved the hot showers and the white, fluffy robes. They admitted to watching "monster movies" on the TV and jumping on the beds. These young women, born into extreme poverty, had now taken their first international flight, slept in a 4-star hotel,

On stage at Inspire

and in a few minutes, would be speaking with me on stage. Over the course of the conference, they met hundreds of women proud to sell the beautiful silver jewelry they created. Our weekend ended with a dance party, and the girls danced, sang, and celebrated with everyone. After the conference, Clare arranged for the girls to spend the day at Disney World before they flew home to Guatemala. The smiles in the photos Clare sent were radiating pure joy.

STAYING CONNECTED

Our annual conferences often provided the momentum we needed to stay connected for the next 11 months. Believe it or not, the greatest challenge to staying connected wasn't always internet accessibility for our Artisan Partners, as you might suspect. It was harnessing the focused energy of our Partners. These mission-minded women worked hard and independently to build their own businesses under the Trades of Hope umbrella.[30] By 2018, we had thousands of Partners at Trades of Hope, which meant we needed a pathway, a process, and a strong home office team to keep everyone and everything *connected*.

For our US Partners, we offered Monday Morning "Wake-Up" calls as our way of giving updates, training, and inspiration from other Partners as their peers. We had different incentives as our "onboarding" process, with fun rewards for the Partners as they started selling our Artisan's products. We created a back office online with a ton of resources and training. Early on, we decided it was important for us to learn and grow together; it was also a top priority to find ways to lift others up through celebration. Those practices brought us closer together and kept up the momentum of a rising tide: learning, growing, and celebrating with each other.

We also started *Kindred,* a blog on our website, where we share Artisan stories—many of these stories told by the women themselves. The blog makes it easy for our Partners to share stories and updates with friends and family who have questions about Trades of Hope or the purpose behind their small businesses.

Elisabeth and I have a podcast for visionary women called *Legacy.* It's been so much fun creating this together. We discuss practical lifestyle and success tips meant to encourage you to get out of your own way as you pursue your big dreams. We talk about everything from how to grow your confidence to women and money. We love when women do things they never thought possible, and this is our way of encouraging that growth.

Our annual conferences and extra events are special ways we stay connected. They are also exhilarating and exhausting! But we look forward to planning the next one as soon as the last one is over. However, as I write this book, we're already thinking "outside the box" about easier ways to gather women in a post-COVID world. So we're focusing on hosting local meetups for deeper community and connection. I think if anything, a pandemic has shown the world how powerful connecting in person is to us individually, but also to inspire activity within organizations.

Corporate giving became a priority for staying connected as well by giving 10% of our corporate profits back in meaningful ways to our Artisan Partners and their surrounding communities. Over the years, this has looked like donating bikes and birthing kits, already mentioned, and—another favorite donation—providing thousands of Plumpy'Nut[31] packets as therapeutic sources of nutrition for malnourished children in 60 countries around the world. And as a way of staying connected to needs in our own communities, in 2021, we partnered with Rebecca Bender's organization, Elevate Academy, to support women in the US coming out of trafficking situations. Elevate Academy is an innovative online school for survivors of human trafficking. The classes focus on professional development and economic empowerment that are designed to help survivors in the next steps towards a new start to life.

These are just a few ways we stay connected, inside and outside of our organization.

DEFINING SUCCESS

One more thing that makes me feel so proud of the "outside the box" ways we've built our company is our mindset around incentives. Instead of extravagant gifts, cash rewards, and tropical trips (as is customary for other direct sales companies), our top-selling Partners earn things like cleft-palate surgeries for children in Guatemala, sewing machines for an Artisan group in India, or sponsorship of a little girl in Haiti to go to school. And the best part is, they *love* earning (or *giving*) these incentives! Our Partners have always carried the mindset that if they were successful in their businesses, then the Artisan Partners would be successful in their businesses, too. They have always wanted to make a positive impact in the world.

IMAGINING THE POSSIBILITIES

When it comes to using ethical fashion to alleviate poverty, there will always be more possibilities to imagine and more ways to think outside of the box. Yet these things will always remain true about Trades of Hope as long as Elisabeth and I are at the helm:

Our Fair Trade Guarantee. As members of the Fair Trade Federation, our styles are made in safe working conditions, and all Artisans are paid living wages for their region. In fact, Artisans are paid 100% of their asking price before their design or product is released online.

Our Mission to Alleviate Poverty and Stop Human Trafficking. Of the Artisans we work with in over 15 countries, generally, 80% are women and 20% are men. Statistically, when you empower one woman to move out of poverty, she takes four other people with her.[32]

Gifts of Hope. We are committed to corporate generosity by donating 10% of our net profits to life-changing causes in and around our Artisan Partner communities. Trades of Hope customers and their purchases directly impact our ability to give to causes such as education, counseling, natural disaster relief, sustainable agriculture, and fighting human trafficking.

This is the incredible work we can do because of a strong company vision and mission-minded women like you around the world. This is the difference we're making *together* at Trades of Hope.

Chapter Nine

THE SEARCH FOR PARTNERS

Start with Dignity

IN 2021, ELISABETH AND I were on a Forbes list of founders and business mentors, an honor we worked hard to earn. Writer Monica Burns published a segment highlighting us in a Forbes article titled "Got Goals? Time to Get a Coach."[33]

> *Mother and daughter CEO team, Elisabeth and Gretchen Huijskens, built their company for the sake of empowering women across the globe in hopes of eliminating poverty and trafficking, while creating job opportunities. Through their business model, they help women start their own businesses and provide sales training by selling fair-trade clothing and jewelry from women around the globe working to keep their children out of poverty, trafficking and orphanages.*

In Elisabeth's spare time, she started offering career coaching to help females reach their entrepreneurial or traditional career goals. She also began creating more training and coaching groups within Trades of Hope. I was honored to be recognized by Forbes as a business mentor, and yet, my focus always leans more toward finding ways to help mothers keep their children through job creation.

Just a few years earlier, in 2017-2018, we did an in-depth survey of our organization and realized we were working with over 10,000 full-time and part-time Partners and Artisan Partners—mostly women. Additionally, it was estimated that our Artisan Partner communities were supporting tens of thousands more people—individuals were receiving health care and clean water and children were being educated.[34] These numbers were incredible!

Behind these incredible numbers were stories of women and their families whose lives had been transformed by a job. It wasn't just the job that made the difference—it was all the things that came with the job: a fair wage, safe working conditions, a supportive community, and a sisterhood. Joining an Artisan Partner group has not only been life-changing for these women, it's been life-*saving* for many of them, too. Many Artisans come from communities where they have been ignored and oppressed. For that very reason, we are protective of their stories—how we request their stories and how those stories are shared. We try not to speak on behalf of these women but work hard to create a platform for them to share their stories using their own voices at their own will when they're ready to do so. Even our product packaging includes messages quoted directly from the Artisans. Our mission is to create dignified partnerships between Trades of Hope, our Partners, our Artisan Partners, and our customers. We believe when women have healthy, supportive work relationships built on dignity and integrity, they become the heroes of their own stories. This is the Trades of Hope sisterhood.

ARTISAN PARTNER STORIES

Our Artisan Partners come from 15-plus countries on four continents. They are real women rising out of poverty every day with the help of people like you and me. On average, our Artisan Partners are 80% women and 20% men. And many, if not all, are supporting their immediate families as well as their extended families. They long for the security of a consistent income. They want to make sure their families are safe, fed, housed, educated, and have access to medical care when needed. Many of us take these most basic things for granted in the US, but they are not always as accessible in places where these women work and live. These Artisans are the reason for our vision and mission. As I often say to our home team, *"We can sell anything, but for Trades of Hope, it's about the people behind each product."*

As we collect stories from Artisans willing to share, it's easy to get overwhelmed with the problems of poverty. You may feel a twinge of that when hearing their stories. But I'll remind you of the same thing I remind myself regularly: *we can't all work to fix everything all at once.* Atrocities are going on in the world constantly. Many of them are the effects of persistent poverty. And many of those atrocities can be turned around with sustainable solutions over time. It is a long game, but it is full of hope.

Here are some stories of the people, places, and products made where our Artisan Partner groups are located. The personal stories I'm about to share were collected by our Artisan communications department and approved by the Artisans themselves:

AFRICA

In **Kenya**, nearly 44 million men, women, and children live in extreme poverty. Starvation, malnutrition, and poor healthcare are common and lead to many congenital disabilities. Because some Kenyans are superstitious and believe disabilities are caused by evil witchcraft, babies born with disabilities are often abandoned, especially if they're little girls. Pressure for mothers to commit infanticide or abandon their disabled infants can be overwhelming. As adults, these individuals are rejected by society, making it hard to find work to support themselves and their families. Profits made by our Artisan Partner groups in Kenya support a community center where women living with disabilities in extreme poverty can find a job in a safe working environment. The center is also home to its very own Artisan community.

The Artisan group was created years before by Mennonite missionary women in the region of Mombasa, Kenya. These beautiful men and women were ostracized from their families, their loved ones, and their communities at large, and this center is now their safe haven. Today, the workshop—tucked behind a wall in a beautiful, well-manicured garden—provides job training and employment for 150 Artisans with physical disabilities. This training allows the Artisans to earn an income for themselves and their families in a dignified way. Because of opportunities within this community, they now have access to safe housing, health care, education, and counseling.

The Story of Alice:

Alice knows firsthand the struggles of disabled women in Kenya. Born a healthy little girl, her mother began to notice delays in her developmental milestones after her first birthday. At one-and-a-half years old, Alice still could not walk and struggled to maintain a healthy weight. Doctors discovered that brittle bone disease was causing her spine to curve, damaging her nerves and causing her to lose the use of her legs. As Alice grew, her challenges of overcoming her culture's discrimination against women with disabilities grew as well. When her disability prevented her from attending college, she faced an uncertain future.

"I was unhappy and discouraged. I didn't know where my meal would come from." Now, thanks to the Artisan community, Alice feels hopeful, "Now I feel free. I feel like a person!"

With the use of a motorized wheelchair, she can be safe, secure, and live a full life. For individuals like Alice, wheelchairs provide mobility and independence in ways they've never known.

Unable to have biological children, crafting jewelry has empowered Alice to create a family of her own. As an Artisan Partner, she earns enough income to provide food, shelter, clothing, and education for herself, her adopted daughter, and her orphaned niece. She even saves money and dreams of owning her own business one day.

Today, Alice's Artisan group employs 37 disabled Artisans, impacting over 100 children receiving an education directly from Artisan benefits. All 37 Artisans receive healthcare benefits, including the 20 artisans who work only part-time. To many of the disabled women in Alice's community, the greatest benefit of becoming an Artisan Partner is a renewed sense of purpose. Purchasing jewelry from Kenya directly impacts the lives of women with disabilities in Alice's community.

Elisabeth and Gretchen with Artisan Partners in Mombasa, Kenya

In 2018, Elisabeth, Frits, Harrison, Mia, and I flew into Nairobi and took the train to Mombasa. *Am I the only one who thinks a train ride to Mombasa sounds exotic and dreamy?* It was an interesting ride—not nearly the fun, romantic experience I made up in my mind. But we had a lovely time experiencing the unique coastal culture. There were beautiful sandy beaches with camels covered in brightly colored woven materials, led by men offering rides to the tourists. The area has a very strong Indian influence, so I was thrilled to see savory curry dishes on every menu. As much as I loved the scenery and the food, by far, the highlight of visiting Mombasa was the time we spent with the Artisans. We had been working together for years, but this was the first time we had been able to meet them in person. When we pulled through the gates of the Artisan community from the chaotic streets filled with vendors, school kids, and too many cars, it was like entering a secret garden. The people were so warm and welcoming. There were many introductions to make, followed by a tour of the whole compound. An elaborate display of food and dinner entertainment from local performers waited for us. After a warm welcome, a delicious meal, and some time getting to know one another, they led us to their makeshift conference room. The accountant in the group sat us down and started reading off our history of sales and declining purchase orders. He provided copies to each of us so we could follow along. The bottom line: our purchase orders had declined, and they were wondering why.

"What have we done that sales are declining? Is the quality not good? Are we charging too much?"

We had worked with them long enough that they noticed when product demands dipped according to declining sales at our end.

In reality, we rounded up their prices to pay them more than they were charging us at times, but their products simply were not selling fast enough at Trades of Hope for us to make consistent purchase orders. I looked at Elisabeth and Frits with tears in my eyes to see they had tears in their eyes, too. I turned back to the leader and said in a reassuring tone,

"We love what you're doing. You make beautiful jewelry. Our whole business is slowing down; it's not just you."

But I am sure that this visit improved their purchase orders, as Elisabeth and I completely fell in love with the mission of this group and all of the people working there. Whenever possible, we always try to encourage their designs and include new pieces from them in our Trades of Hope line.

Another fun tidbit about this group was they were always thinking of creative ways to come up with product development solutions, including creating menu covers for the hotel where we stayed while we were in town. Most of our Artisan Partner groups had this kind of creative ingenuity—proof that these women could think and act like business entrepreneurs once they were no longer in survival mode.

Capability is not what they were lacking, which was obvious when they were simply given an opportunity.

In **Uganda**, our Artisan Partner groups are made up of refugees and marginalized women living in the slums. Jobs created within these communities give women access to dignified employment, health care, and clean water. Many families in Uganda have been displaced from their ancestral homes by war, extreme poverty, lack of education and job opportunities, and discrimination. As a result, they face homelessness and starvation. But Ugandan women are leading their families out of poverty by creating traditional art and jewelry using Artisan skills passed down for generations.

Elisabeth and I had the opportunity to travel to Uganda to meet with our Artisan Partner groups. One of these groups was led by a woman named Florence.

The Story of Ms. Florence:

Florence is a matriarch in her community. As a war refugee, Florence wanted to provide more for her family and community. She has inspired so many women in the slums of Uganda by giving them the tools to make an income and have hope for their future. They're now able to afford better living conditions and medical expenses, and send their children to school. Florence shared with us that many of these women are understanding their worth for the first time as they experience the joy of dignified work!

In Her Own Words:
"Before I started working with Trades of Hope, I used to live hand to mouth. I was dependent on my brothers for house rent, school fees for my son, and medical bills. But

that changed when I started working with Trades of Hope.
I'm now self-reliant. I've acquired assets like land and even
constructed a house in the village. I have access to better
medical care, and I pay my own medical bills! I'm also able
to support other vulnerable relatives and people from the
community. I'm stress-free and not worried about the future
anymore!"

Meeting Florence was a highlight of our trip to Uganda. The women in her community loved her, and it isn't hard to understand why. She is vivacious, kind, and strong. And she treats everyone she meets with care and dignity. One afternoon, Florence, Elisabeth, and I took a walk through the local shanty village. (This is the photo on the cover of this book.) In between hugging and greeting people, she shared openly

Gretchen, Florence, Elisabeth with kids
from the village

with us about how difficult it was to be a woman in Uganda. Florence
shared that many women and their young families lived in crowded
slums with no access to job opportunities, quality education, clean
water, electricity, or sanitary drainage. In their community, they had

many teenage mothers who could not find good jobs because of their low level of education and older women with aids or disabilities who also had no way to earn a living.

Florence took us to meet one of the Artisans in her home. The woman was so welcoming, with a vibrant personality. She invited us inside, and we sat on the floor of her one-room house to talk. This woman was so proud to tell us her story of arriving in this village with her young daughter and nothing else. After meeting Florence and joining the Artisan Partner group, she found the home she was in now, but it was completely empty. She and her daughter slept on grass mats in the little house those first weeks. But now she was thrilled to show us how she had earned enough income to buy a beautiful bed for the two of them, a small refrigerator, and a boombox to play music. Now she could sing and dance again. But the best thing of all was her ability to pay her daughter's school fees on a consistent basis. Florence shared with us that many of the women we have partnered with as Artisans understand their worth for the first time in their lives as they experience the joy of dignified work.

ASIA

In **Cambodia**, the Artisan group we worked with was essentially started by one resilient young woman called Ya. Ya was a survivor of an acid attack, as were many of the women in the group with her. Acid was often a man's way of keeping his wife in line. The physical effects and lasting stigma were eternally damaging to the reputation and cultural position of every victim. But Ya was spunky, strong, and had a huge heart to help other women like her who had been recovering from the same type of hatred. An American woman named Wendy found Ya in the hospital while visiting other friends. Wendy and Ya became instant friends. Not only did Wendy take Ya under her wing and love her like her family, but—when Ya was ready—Wendy emailed Trades of Hope to see if there was something Ya could make to earn an income with us as an Artisan. We've worked together with Ya on different products over the years, and when she has enough orders, Ya includes other survivors as Artisans, too. This opportunity through Ya gives these women income, community, and purpose. These women now had the chance to rediscover hope and dignity as Artisans and independent businesswomen.

In 2015, Frits and I were visiting Angkor Wat in Siem Reap, Cambodia, and had the opportunity to fly 50 minutes south to Phnom Penh to spend a day with Ya. We were so close and didn't want to miss the opportunity to meet and spend time with this incredible person. We arrived in Phnom Penh at about noon. Ya came to pick us up in a tuk-tuk—a small motorized rickshaw with three wheels—a very common source of transportation in the region. The small cart received its interesting name because of the "ticking" sound made by the small two-cycle engine. Ya was a bubbly twenty-something

Gretchen and Ya riding in a tuk-tuk

wearing bright-blue eyeshadow with dark hair dyed red. She was so excited we were there to visit, and she talked nonstop from the moment we hugged hello. Ya wore a mask over her nose and mouth to cover her scarred face, but she took it off at times when she was making a point regarding something she said.

Ya took us around town for several hours, introducing us to some women she wanted us to meet. The first two women we visited lived just outside the city. These women were bonded by their similar experiences of being acid attack survivors. The wind blew hard as we drove 30 minutes outside the city limits to visit these women, and I remember Ya chatting the whole way. It was delightful! As we pulled up to the chain-linked fence alongside the road, the three women greeted each other. One of them even welcomed us into her home for tea. They were warm and friendly, and we tried our best to get to know each other with Ya as our translator. Since their acid attacks, these women had been working at a local hospital cleaning at night. It was the only work they could find since everyone thought they were cursed because of the "bad Karma" that followed them. Even as they worked at night, people would kick them and spit on them as they walked by. It was hard to hear their stories, but their warmth and hospitality inspired us. About two hours later, we climbed back into the tuk-tuk to drive back into the city.

On the way, Ya told me about the last time she was in the hospital recovering from one of several reconstructive surgeries that she needed to open up her ears and nose after the attack. Seeing Ya in pain with tears rolling down her cheek, an older woman came over to comfort her. She said to Ya,

"There, there. Not to worry. Whatever you did in your past lives, you are paying for now, so your next life should be very good."

Ya knew she had done nothing to deserve that attack, but that's not what most people thought when they looked at her. Not only were these survivors dealing with pain that never really went away, there was also the pain of their community telling them they were "bad" people. This broke my heart for Ya and her friends.

The last stop of the day was deep into the city. It was dark at this point, and I hoped we weren't being naive riding around Phnom Penh in an open tuk-tuk that late. We pulled up to a labyrinth of cement blocks—one-room homes connected by extremely narrow alleys. Ya led us quickly down one of these long alleys. A few steps in, I realized what we were doing wasn't smart at all. We could be trapped from the front and behind. But it was too late now. At this point, there was little to do but to follow Ya. Music blasted from a few homes, and some of the doorways were loud with yelling. Finally, we stepped into the home of a young mom. It was obvious she was caring for her children on her own. She, too, had scars from acid. And like Ya, she was beautiful with a sweet spirit. We sat down on mats laid out on her cement floor. This wise young woman told us about her life, showed us a photo of her beautiful 3-year-old daughter, and then showed us the crocheted products she was making for Trades of Hope. We sat and talked while Ya translated for about 30 minutes, then hugged goodbye and went back into the alleys. Ya said we had another stop to make, so we had to keep moving.

It was a quick walk to our next stop. This woman we met was another acid attack victim, probably around my age. She was so happy to see Ya and immediately welcomed us into her home. She had a four-year-old daughter who also had some burns on her face and arms. The woman's husband threw acid on her because he said she "disobeyed" him. When it happened, she cried out in pain, causing her daughter to run and wrap her arms around her mother. The daughter was also deformed from the acid to the point where she could no longer attend school because of how horribly the other children treated her. But she was making the best of her circumstances.

After the last visit, Ya dropped us off at the Foreign Correspondence Hotel for the night. I looked forward to staying there because of the history of the building. It was an old French-colonial mansion that sat on the promenade where the Mekong and Tonlé Sap Rivers converge. The hotel had become a temporary home to expat reporters and photographers during the Cambodian-Vietnamese War. I remember sitting on the infamous terrace overlooking the river at the hotel restaurant that evening, and I could barely stomach the lovely fried rice in front of me. I replayed everything we saw earlier that day. Frits and I just sat in silence, looking out over the city. Cambodia was beautiful, but the poverty we experienced was devastating.

The next morning, Ya picked us up for another day of introductions and touring. We visited another acid attack survivor in the hospital. Her attack happened in the market where she rented a stall and sold handmade goods. Apparently, the goods and products she carried were similar to another woman's goods and products just a few stalls away, and the other woman was not happy about it. So, the stall owner hired someone to throw acid on her. The police were bribed to side with the angry stall owner, and the case was closed without justice for the survivor. And now, here was this innocent woman, lying on her stomach in a hospital bed with open wounds on her back and legs. She was suffering so much that tears streamed down her face in a steady roll from the constant pain. Her loving husband stood at the end of her bed and gently rubbed her feet, as that was the only place he could touch without causing more pain.

I still don't completely understand why Ya wanted me to meet all of these women. Some we worked with through Trades of Hope, but some we didn't. I guess she wanted me to see the need for job creation, particularly for these women. She definitely gave me a crash course in the realities of being a woman in a culture so different from my own. I'm grateful that we have been able to offer job opportunities for Ya, and my hope is we can eventually do so much more for many more survivors like her.

The Story of Ya: *In Her Own Words*

"My name is Jariya. One day someone flung a container of acid in my face. It burned my face, and ran down my body, dissolving both my skin and my life. The excruciating extensive burns threatened to take my life for months, and since then, I've had to endure numerous surgeries to attempt to re-make my features and face to be normal again. I now have to live with the scarring on my face and body and also with the scarring on my heart. I've consistently been the subject of mockery, hatred, rejection, and curiosity, but rarely the subject of compassion or help. I'm gradually trying to rebuild my life and make a future for myself. But the only thing that gives me the courage to do that is that I know that I'm not alone and that I may be able to do something to help others. I started a family with my husband Seth. We have a baby boy, and his name is Pratana. Without support from Trades of Hope, I wouldn't be able to have a family. Life would be difficult, and I would suffer from hunger. And it brings me great encouragement. It's started to wash away all the words that people used to speak over me and my life."

Later that day, we flew back to Siem Reap to meet up with the rest of our touring crew. I have to admit, I was relieved to leave. After our plane landed, our tuk-tuk driver asked if we minded him taking a shortcut. With my mind still on Ya, I said, "Sure. No problem." Siem Reap is a beautiful place with nice hotels and manicured roadsides that all lead to ancient temples. It felt so serene and peaceful. But our shortcut off the main road would reveal extreme poverty behind the beautiful main street veneer. It added to the images we had seen with Ya earlier that day in Phnom Penh. The side street was lined with homes made of corrugated metal sheets, tree branches, and tarps. Women were cooking over open fires, and small children were wandering naked very close to the road. There wasn't anything peaceful and serene on that street, just one block away from the main street. It felt heavy and oppressive.

As we came to the end of the street, on the right side was a huge white wall the length of the whole block. The driver made a right turn and another right, and there we were in front of the 5-star Sofitel Hotel. We pulled through the gates into a lush, manicured garden with men in clean, crisp uniforms to greet us. In a matter of seconds, we traveled through two very different extremes: on one side, extreme poverty, and on the other side, the high-end hotel where we gathered with the rest of our group for lunch. It was jarring, to say the least.

Frits and I got out of the tuk-tuk, determined to set all of the hard stuff aside and have a nice lunch with our group. We found them sitting at a large table on a patio surrounded by shaded gardens. It was incredibly beautiful and smelled of jasmine. When they saw us, they welcomed us, pointed to the seats they saved around the table, then asked about our trip. Our trip leader, John, said, "So, how was it in Phnom Penh? Tell us all about it!" Frits and I both answered something to the effect of, "Well, it really isn't good lunch conversation." We were trying hard to steer the topic in another direction, but the group was kind and persistent. So we began to tell them what we saw. Both Frits and I cried as we told them about the women we had met—survivors of acid attacks. Ya and her friends were amazing women, but what they went through, and continued to go through, was heartbreaking in every way. We told them about the woman lying face-down in her hospital bed, crying tears of pain. And my own tears flowed even harder. Then, to top it all off, we shared what we saw on the other side of the huge white wall at the end of the patio courtyard where we all sat for lunch. By the end, my chest ached.

Well . . . we really knew how to bring down a room (or a patio, in this case). We apologized, but the group thanked us for sharing these experiences with them. After lunch, the group was going to visit another area of Siem Reap, but Frits and I needed more time. The day before, when we flew to meet Ya in Phnom Penh, the group had gone to the Raffles Hotel to have high tea in the conservatory. The historic hotel, with its French Art Deco design, opened its doors in 1932. It was the temporary home to glamorous people of the world who visited Angkor Wat, but also a place of negotiations during tur- bulent times. Like the Foreign Correspondence Hotel, the history was intriguing, but the beautiful environment of the conservatory was soothing. It was essentially a sunroom with a view over the gar- dens and pool, classically decorated with large, comfortable sofas and chairs, embroidered throw pillows, and blooming white orchids. This is where Frits and I landed that afternoon. We missed high tea, so we ordered two of the famous Singapore Sling cocktails and sat close together in silence. At one point, we started laughing with tears in our eyes because the past 24 hours just seemed so crazy. In one day, we had seen enough human suffering to last a lifetime. We were feel- ing overwhelmed and a bit lost, sitting in this really expensive hotel, dusty from the tuk-tuks, eyes swollen from crying, with huge cock- tails in our hands—fruit and flowers coming out of the top of each glass. We were quite the sight! We talked about how we wanted to do more for these women. We wanted Ya to be able to help more women find hope through dignified partnerships with Trades of Hope.

And there's more.

In **India**, our Artisan Partner communities make it possible to stop the exploitation of vulnerable women in sweatshops thanks to fair-trade jobs in areas of extreme poverty. These communities also work to prevent child marriage, a common practice in the region. Our Artisan Partners in India are committed to preserving India's time-honored leather-crafting traditions while advocating for women's equality and supporting education for children in rural villages. Their ancient leather-crafting and block-printing techniques turn into beautiful traditional designs with modern functions. Their leather bags are some of our customer favorites. And every purchase supports these beautiful women and their families.

Stories of women being cast out of communities because husbands or fathers threw acid on them are just as common in India as in other parts of East Asia. These women are now disabled, or differently abled, and yet they are still beautiful and determined to work on creating their designs. Dressed in colorful traditional Indian saris and sitting in rows of stitching machines and worktables covered with materials, each woman has her own inspiring story of hope, her own personal story of overcoming extreme challenges to create a new life for herself and her family. One woman is learning to use a sewing machine with one hand after she was burned for a dowry. Another woman was accidentally electrocuted and lost much of the feeling in her hands. Nearby is a young man who is considered "unemployable" by most local employers because of his learning disabilities. But the consistent and repetitive nature of his work has helped him become an accomplished Artisan. He enjoys this opportunity to express his personal creativity, and he takes pride in creating his products with excellence.

The Story of Dilshad:

Growing up, Dilshad studied until 10th-grade standard. Like many young girls in India, once she discontinued her schooling, her parents arranged her marriage. Soon after the birth of her son, her husband's attitude toward her changed. His family wanted money to buy a goods trolley, and they pressured Dilshad to get the money from her parents. But Dilshad's father was a taxi driver and couldn't have spared the amount of money they wanted. When she refused to ask her parents for the money, her in-laws began to physically torture her and threatened her for over a year. When Dilshad complained to her husband, he refused to believe her. Dilshad knew her life was in danger, but she was afraid to tell her parents because her story was so disturbing. She finally reached out for help from some of her neighbors, who offered their sympathy but did nothing to help her.

One evening, Dilshad's mother-in-law asked her to prepare tea. So, Dilshad lit the stove and put a pan of water on it, completely unaware that her mother-in-law was sneaking up behind her with a can of kerosene oil. As Dilshad added milk and tea powder to the boiling water, her mother-in-law emptied the can of kerosene all over Dilshad. Before Dilshad realized what was happening, the fire from the stove engulfed her. She cried for help, but her mother-in-law fled with Dilshad's baby. Neighbors heard her screaming and rushed over to cover her with a blanket. She was taken to the hospital and survived. But her face and hands were no longer the same. Dilshad was forced not to say anything to the police and told them it was an accident.

After her recovery, she went to live with her parents. Her husband and in-laws never came to take her back. Her parents petitioned the local elders to settle out of court, and Dilshad's husband divorced her. That was the end of Dilshad's marital life. In a culture where divorced women and women with disabilities have traditionally been marginalized, Dilshad was now living with the challenge of both social stigmas. But her life was about to change...

In January 2003, Dilshad reached out to a local Artisan community in search of a new beginning. The wounds on her hands had not even healed yet. Unable to work, she was asked to return when her wounds were healed. Six months later, she returned and began training to become an Artisan. Since then, she has never looked back.

In Her Own Words:
"When I came to this workshop, the wounds on my hands were still raw. I couldn't lift or hold anything. It took me four

to five years to learn everything. Whatever samples I get, I'm capable of making now. There is immense joy in working with everyone. They showed me a new direction in life. In the aftermath of what happened to me, I was so confused. I didn't know how to start afresh—how to groom my child. They kindled new hopes in my shattered life and gave it a new meaning. I've got something that is more than a family here! Here, I work with dignity and hard work. This Artisan community has helped me enormously! I didn't take anyone's help to educate my son. I did it myself."

Like Dilshad, each woman in her Artisan community is learning to write a new ending to a tragic story that could have left them destitute. But now Dilshad is teaching them—not only Artisan skills that will help them provide for themselves and their families—but also how to overcome their challenges and become equal partners and active leaders in their communities.

In **Nepal**, our Artisan Partner groups help women overcome gender discrimination and sex trafficking by providing dignified jobs with fair wages. Women are empowered with equal opportunities to enjoy creating decor from felt and beautiful-yet-practical knitted pieces such as scarves and mittens as well as ornaments using traditional felting techniques.

In the **Philippines**, our Artisan Partner groups provide fair-trade jobs in remote villages so parents can stay with their families and not have to travel far and live elsewhere to earn a fair wage. Finding employment as a woman in poverty can be extremely difficult in the Philippines. Poor working conditions, lack of job security, and unfair pay are often the realities. Through the purchase of their handcrafted designs, women who become Artisans receive income, health care, and social development programs. This allows these women to realize their potential and pursue their dreams in a safe environment.

Retchel from The Philippines

In **Thailand**, it's much the same. Artisan Partner groups allow moms to work near their families, often in remote villages, so they can be home with their kids and send them to school. The women from our Artisan Partner group in Thailand make beautiful beadwork. The workshop there was founded by a local woman named Aoi, who had witnessed too many women in Thailand's rural villages be forced to leave their children behind to find jobs in the city so they could send money home to feed their children. So, she created a workshop to offer skills training, business mentoring, scholarships for Artisans' children, emergency health care coverage, micro-loan programs, and job flexibility that allows women like Aoi to also work from home. Every purchase of Trades of Hope designs from Thailand supports this rural village workshop and helps these women help their families prosper.

In **Vietnam**, our Artisan Partner groups help women overcome gender discrimination by providing job skills training and local fair-trade jobs. In recent decades, Vietnam has made commendable strides in improving social and economic conditions for women and families rising out of poverty. But there are still many women and children in areas of extreme poverty in Vietnam who live with the lingering stigma created by centuries of discrimination against women. A lack of education—especially for girls—makes children growing up in poverty even more vulnerable to homelessness and exploitation. Children whose families can't afford to pay the fees for them to attend quality schools often struggle in adulthood to find employment that provides enough income to support a family with basic essentials. In addition to women, persons with disabilities and homeless individuals also face cultural discrimination that hinders them from securing safe, dignified housing and employment. Trades of Hope is partnering with Artisan communities in Vietnam, who are providing life-changing opportunities for these oppressed people to rise.

In other areas of **East Asia**, one Artisan group helps survivors of sex trafficking experience hope and healing through dignified job opportunities, trauma counseling, and education. We got connected to these Artisans through a nonprofit organization for survivors of human trafficking. The organization offers a 3-year leadership development pathway for women. I love every time I get to talk to Jenny, the founder of the project, and hear the stories of these women. Not only do they provide practical life skills and job training for these women, but they also do kind things for them, too. One time, I was on a call catching up with Jenny, and she told me that she'd been busy in her office, working on spreadsheets and budgets (all of the fun stuff, not really). She said she had been feeling stressed and frustrated when someone knocked on her door to tell her they were going to celebrate the birthday of a new woman in their program. This was a tradition Jenny started years ago. But with so many women, it felt like they were always singing and eating cake. Jenny dropped what she was doing and went downstairs. They brought out the cake and sang, but they also did what they always do—they went around the room so everyone could say one nice thing about the woman they were celebrating. After the last person to share, the young woman broke down in tears. She thanked them and said it was the first time anyone had ever celebrated her birthday. Jenny told me that those times were the important little reminders she needed to keep focused on their true mission. These women needed their freedom and help in developing their careers, but they also needed to be valued and loved.

Two of our Artisan Partners in East Asia

Zi Yun: *In her own words*

I grew up in a poor family and was the youngest of nine kids. I had to quit elementary school so that I could sell eggs to help support my family.

By the time I was 15 I had been married and abandoned by my husband. I had nowhere to go. I tried to work at a restaurant, but I couldn't even write down what people ordered. With no education or options, a friend brought me to a brothel. I worked in brothels for many years and eventually ran my own. I recruited girls into the brothels myself until a team shared with me the story of hope and everything began to change.

After receiving healing in my own life, I began to have a burden for the women and girls still working in the brothels. Today because of my belief and the love of the people around me, I go into the same neighborhoods filled with brothels that I used to work in so that I can bring women and girls out of the dark life of exploitation and help them experience true freedom.

CARIBBEAN

In the **Dominican Republic**, our Artisan Partner groups help women break free from poverty, including domestic abuse and human trafficking, through dignified job opportunities in safe workplaces and counseling.

In 2019, we met an English woman living in the DR. Katie originally came to the US, earned an architectural degree and traveled to the DR on a work trip to help the locals build homes. While working there, Katie fell in love with the country and the people. She also saw an opportunity. The longer Katie lived in the DR, the more her eyes were opened to the plight of many women around her. Not only were women being treated poorly by the men in rural island communities, but they were being trafficked, too. Katie eventually put together a small home called Casa Azul for women who were rescued from sex trafficking and mandated by the court system to find a safe place to live away from their abusers.

When we visited Katie in 2019, Frits and I stayed at a lovely eco-lodge at the top of the hill from Casa Azul. Katie picked us up for a tour the next morning. As we drove around the region, she pointed out small motel-like structures that dotted the roadside. These motels had two stories—the first story was a standard-sized car garage, with motel room quarters on the second floor. Katie told us how these motels made it easy for men to bring young women in for their "services" without being seen in public. They could pull into the garage, shut the door, and take the women upstairs. Many of them were underage and doing this against their own will. *This was human trafficking.* And it was happening throughout the countryside. People were making huge profits building these motels all over the DR.

It wasn't unusual to hear stories of teenage girls who gave birth to their father's children. Many of these girls were no more than 11 or 12 years old—a reality no child should ever have to endure. We met a young woman named Yocasta, who gave birth to three children by the time she was 19. Yocasta had been abused and sold into slavery by her own father, who had done the same thing to another sister. It was due to really hard situations that girls and women were rescued and placed in the safety of Casa Azul.

Back at the eco-lodge that night, after a day with Katie, we had a hard time finishing our dinner now that we knew what was *really* going on just down the hill. Both Frits and I knew this was an Artisan Partner community we wanted to help. To be able to sell the items these young women were making would be an honor. We wanted to help Katie help these women transition into happier, healthier seasons of their lives.

Today, Katie is recognized as an expert in rescuing young girls and women from human trafficking. She works with government officials, local police, and an anti-trafficking organization called Operation Rescue Mission. The last time I checked in with her, she was excited to share that her local community had a new female police chief. Katie was excited to start working with her to help more women and girls.

In **Haiti**, we help mothers provide and care for their children, so they won't have to give their babies up as poverty orphans to orphanages. We work with Artisans making beaded jewelry out of cereal boxes and clay. And we work with Artisans from the community of Croix du Bouquet, where beautiful metalwork is created out of discarded steel drums. Haitians make everything out of these drums, from crosses used as grave markers to elaborate family tree cut-outs to mark their history and remember their heritage. Most of the drums were used to transport imported oil to Haiti. A ready supply of these 55-gallon drums was available after they had been emptied. An Artisan in the 1950s started cutting the steel to shape it into crosses to honor the dead in cemeteries. This is how a whole Artisan community was formed at Croix du Bouquet (translation: *bouquet of crosses*). Now it is a thriving business with hundreds of Artisans, still using chalk to trace out the shapes from cardboard templates and then simple hammers and chisels to create the designs. It's truly remarkable.

We took a group of Partners to Haiti one year to meet the Artisans who made the jewelry and metalwork we sold at Trades of Hope. The Artisans, who were part of the Artisan community where my friend

Shelley worked, agreed to teach our Partners how to roll cereal box beads and work with clay. As the Partners and Artisans paired up around work tables, I walked around the make sure everyone had a place to sit. As I was walking, I noticed a group of women talking and crying—an unusual public expression of emotion for these Haitian women. I heard one of the Haitian Artisan Partners via a translator ask Stacie, from our Trades of Hope staff,

"Why do you care about this stuff?"

Stacie pulled out a picture of her family on her phone and showed it to the group. She said,

"When we sell your products, it helps you put food on the table for your family and helps me put food on the table for my family, too!"

That's why everyone was in tears. (Thank goodness!) I thought to myself, *that's also something charity can't do*. Charity couldn't create opportunities for sustainable living at both ends of the supply chain. And both women could be proud of what they were doing together! Only development could do that.

Artisans assembling bracelets in Haiti

The Story of Gena:

My friend Shelley, who founded and leads our Artisan Partners in Haiti, shared the story of a young woman named Gena. Shelley heard about a woman named Gena who was wandering the neighborhood asking for an orphanage to drop off her baby girl Chrisnaly because she could no longer feed her. Gena was afraid Chrisnaly would starve, and she wanted to save her baby. She thought an orphanage was her only option. One day, Shelley went out to find Gena, and when she did, she asked Gena, "How about instead, you come and work with us rolling beads? This way, you can earn money and put Chrisnaly in the daycare we offer." Gena looked the part of poverty—her skin aged well beyond her youthful years, and her figure was thin and malnourished. Gena looked miserable and defeated. But she agreed to give the beads a try. I happened to be there with a group of Trades of Hope Partners visiting on Gena's first day and saw how desperate she looked. When I came back the following year, I asked Shelley about Gena and Chrisnaly. She waved a beautiful young lady over to us, and standing there in front of me was Gena! She didn't even look the same. I looked back at Shelly in disbelief, "No, it's not!" I said. "Yes, it is!" she replied. Gena started laughing. She thought my reaction to her change was hilarious. She was beaming with confidence as she held her head high with pride. Then Shelley pointed out Gena's healthy little girl at the Artisan community daycare. Gena embodied a sense of agency—her own agency—now that she had moved past poverty and could provide for herself and her Chrisnaly. The Partners who made that trip with us have been some of our most committed, longstanding Partners because of their experience in Haiti early on with Trades of Hope. Being there in person, these women caught the Trades of Hope vision in ways our mission and our manifesto could never describe.

CENTRAL AMERICA

In **Guatemala**, our Artisan Partner groups create job opportunities in areas of extreme poverty. One of our communities is connected to a safe house for girls overcoming poverty, abuse, and trafficking. Although Guatemala has grown economically in recent years, it still claims one of the highest inequality rates in Latin America. With some of the worst poverty, malnutrition, and maternal-child mortality rates in the region, there is still work to be done before women are treated fairly. That's where Trades of Hope comes in. We work with several Artisan groups to help these women rise above their circumstances.

On my first trip to Guatemala, I met with an American woman named Clare and a few nuns who ran an Artisan Partner group at Casa Hogar. The Home for Children (the English translation for *Casa Hogar*) was a safe house for young girls rescued from abusive and incestuous family situations in remote communities in Guatemala. Clare had been working with the home for a few years, helping them get sewing machines and other resources needed to make local crafts and goods they could sell in Guatemala and abroad. There were about 80 girls living in the home, from toddlers to young women. Most of them stayed in the home until they graduated and were ready to move out on their own. At one point, years before I visited for the first time, Clare asked the nuns, "What do you really need?" The nuns wanted the girls to learn trades they could carry with them beyond the safe house, so they set up a beauty shop and a few sewing machines. The girls learned how to cut and style hair and sew items such as simple backpacks and clothing. Clare began taking these products back to the United States, but they weren't selling so well. So, Clare found a jewelry designer who was willing to come and teach the girls how to make nice silver jewelry. This higher-end jewelry was a fresh idea that included a little silver fingerprint of one of the women making each piece. As a result of learning how to create these unique pieces, these young women now earned a consistent income and had money to spend and save. Clare tells a story about one young woman in the group who went into a store in a nearby town to pick out her own shoes. This was the first time she had gone into a store to choose something for herself. She also purchased the shoes with her *own money*—a first for her. Another young woman bought her own bright blue motorcycle for transportation. For all of these young women, choices like this were so very brave.

When I first saw the jewelry they were making and after a long phone call with Clare, I knew I wanted to add their silver jewelry to our line. Our designer began working with Clare and Skyping with the women in Guatemala to talk about designs. Over the following months, I got to know Clare, and she shared that the young women loved that we wanted to hear their opinions and ideas.

She also shared with me the story of how the silver fingerprints came to be on all of their jewelry. Clare told me sometimes she'd find fingerprints on some of the products she sold to friends in the US. At one point, as a woman purchased a silver bracelet and Clare was handing it to the woman, she noticed a fingerprint and said,

"Hang on, that one has a fingerprint in the silver. Let me find a bracelet that doesn't have prints on it."

And the woman replied, "Oh, even better! I'll take the one with the fingerprints. I love the idea of my bracelet being printed by the Artisan who made it."

And the rest of her friends started looking for other jewelry with fingerprints, too. That's how Clare started fingerprint jewelry. Now the young women add their fingerprints to the silver jewelry *on purpose*. And we love it!

Guatemalan Artisan working on silver fingerprint jewelry

Eventually, Clare would work with the nuns at the safe house to provide additional classes and conversations for the women regarding how to deal with their families after they made their own income. This meant teaching sustainable ways of supporting their families, so they didn't end up in poverty again. One young woman decided to purchase a plot of land for her family to farm so they could grow and sell food rather than just give them money to spend. Money was fleeting, but land and farming were resources that created more job opportunities for more family members. This kind of development mindset was the pathway out of poverty for these young women and their loved ones.

I'll never forget the time Frits traveled to Guatemala with me to meet the girls in this particular Artisan Partner group. Frits was willing to travel along to film stories and capture b-roll for us to share with our Trades of Hope community. The girls were talking about the silver jewelry they were making and showing us some of their pieces on camera. At one point, Frits looked up from filming and said to this group of young women,

"You know you are all international businesswomen now, right?!"

And it was true! These women from rural Guatemala who once lived in extreme poverty were now international businesswomen selling their handmade jewelry all over the world through Trades of Hope and other partnerships. There wasn't a dry eye in the room after Frits called this out.

We started working with other Artisan Partners in Guatemala beyond the group at Casa Hogar. These women came from different regions of Guatemala, where a traditional backstrap loom was used to make the fabric bags we carry online and in our catalogs. It was quite an experience to visit these women on our initial trip as we started working with the group and then went back to see their homes a year or two later. The changes were incredible because these women now earned a livable wage with consistent purchase orders from Trades of Hope and other partnering organizations. Job opportunities through the work of Artisan Partner groups were making their lives so much better.

Two of the women we met, named Martha and Rosa, specialize in upcycling traditional Mayan Huipil fabric into eco-friendly, ethically-made fashions. We briefly touched on this earlier, but I think it's helpful to mention again that Huipil is a beautiful traditional fabric worn by women in Guatemala to signify which village they call home. Each upcycled design they create is one-of-a-kind, as its colors, patterns, and motifs are unique to each woman's village. Many of the trades practiced by these groups—especially weaving, woodworking, pottery, and felt—are cultural techniques and trades passed down from generation to generation.

The Story of Clara, an Artisan in Guatemala:

Clara is a hardworking mother of three who worked in a company outside her city when her children were young. For years, Clara's job kept her from being with her family. As is the struggle of motherhood worldwide, Clara found it increasingly difficult to work outside the home with young children. With the hope of gaining a better work/life balance, she founded the Artisan group with her husband. They built a workshop in their home so she could work with her husband and have more time to spend with her children. This afforded them both the luxury of working out of their home. When other parents from her village still needed to travel far away to earn enough income for their families, Clara decided to help them change their stories by inviting them to work with her. Now Clara could care for and spend time with their children while still providing for the family. It was a blessing that has continued to sustain their little workshop. Their home-based business has now been sewing handicrafts for the past fifteen years. Starting their own workshop meant more than just meeting their needs to balance work and family time: it meant Clara could help others rise out of poverty. She has a big heart for the community and takes a personal interest in those that work for her. They say it takes a village to raise a child, and Clara and her husband exemplify that saying.

Here is how Clara describes her experience in her own words:
"Thank you very much to all of you who are buying our products. We are a group of women who sometimes our husbands have jobs, but other times our husbands don't have jobs. We can bring our kids—little babies—to work with us. It provides us with money every week to feed them. Thank God that we have this help from this partnership! We hope for the future to teach new ladies. We have a lot of requests for other

women to join our Artisan community, but unfortunately, we don't have enough sewing machines."

One of the young women employed by Clara, Mercedes, struggled with abandonment issues from her childhood. Clara and her husband took Mercedes under their wing to help her with food and housing, and Clara taught Mercedes how to sew and make handicrafts. Now that Mercedes is grown, she works in the Artisan group and has the tools she needs to become financially independent.

There are countless more women around the world like Mercedes, desperate to find a way to rise above their circumstances. These women do not want our charity. They want opportunities!

In **Mexico**, our Artisan Partner communities provide jobs with living wages in areas of extreme poverty so moms can send their kids to school instead of sending them to work at a young age. These inspiring women are

Clara in Guatemala

making fair-trade goods by preserving their ancient Aztec and Mayan traditions passed down for generations from their families. These women dye and weave sheep's wool, make jewelry out of amber stone found in Southern Mexico, and create beautiful, handcrafted paper art made from the bark of local trees. Once dependent on tourists to purchase their art in local markets, these women are now reaching a larger market through Trades of Hope in the most sustainable ways.

In **Peru**, women are overcoming poverty with job opportunities. The Artisan community is committed to its mission of keeping the unique jewelry-making techniques and Artisan skills of their Peruvian ancestors alive while helping families rise out of poverty. These Artisans are building and supporting Artisan training centers in remote areas of the jungle where families have few opportunities to earn a living wage.

MIDDLE EAST

In **Jordan**, our communities help marginalized women overcome discrimination and oppression. Women have the opportunity to become financially independent as Artisans. Many of these Artisans in Jordan have lived the majority of their lives completely dependent and controlled by their closest male relative. Lingering influences of ancient traditions and cultural customs have made it difficult for these women to rise above the oppression they've personally experienced. Some of them are divorced, widowed, or married to a man who already has many wives. But amidst their struggles, these women enjoy a family-like workplace as Artisans. Over the years, they've experienced new stories of hope. Now, they can be heard singing, laughing, and drinking tea while creating our unique jewelry from upcycled glass bottles tumbled with water and sand from the Red Sea.

U.S.A.

Here in the US, Trades of Hope partners with stateside Artisan Partner communities for women breaking free from addiction, sex-trafficking, generational poverty, and trauma. These women are rediscovering their value and identity as they're equipped with new skills, independence, and healing. Every purchase of our products from the US empowers a woman to overcome her past and lead her family out of poverty.

THE POWER OF STORIES

Author and entrepreneur Seth Godin says, "People do not buy products and services. They buy relations, stories, and magic." [35] I share these stories here as powerful examples of what happens when women are given an opportunity to step out of poverty with the creation of jobs. If we were simply helping these women by caring for their babies, we would still be doing the good work of saving lives. And yet with job creation opportunities, these women are now empowered to access resources to save their own lives, the lives of their children, and the communities of extended family around them. Our Artisan Partners are literally changing the world, one job at a time! And the same goes for our Partners who are putting food on the table here in the US by selling fair-trade fashion made by their sisters in 15 countries around the world. This is what we call *dignified partnerships*. We are all helping one another make a difference.

Just like the Trades of Hope women—Artisan Partners and Partners—I want you to consider how you've been empowered to make a difference and change the world around you. *What opportunities or invitations have you been given to make life better for you, your children, and your community? What are you actively doing to make a difference—big or small—in the world?*

Chapter Ten

THE RISING TIDE
OF VOICES

Making the Impossible Possible

AS A KID, MY MOM WORKED LONG HOURS to support our family. After work, she spent a few more hours in the car making sure I got to tutoring, piano lessons, dance rehearsal, etc. On top of that, she somehow fulfilled all of my fashion desires. When my kids were little, I realized how hard it must have been to run back out at night and bring me to my various activities after working all day, especially on cold, dark Michigan nights. Once I became a mom and started working hard on my own dreams, I thought about just how proud my mom must have been that she made it possible for us to live a full life of such wonderful opportunities to learn, grow, and develop. And now I get to do the same, not only with my children, but I also get to help mothers keep their children and support them in ways they never dreamed possible. The best part? There's a whole sisterhood of women doing the same for themselves and their families. And this has made all the difference.

When I first started connecting with mamas in Haiti who felt like they had to give up their babies for adoption, I realized I had much more in common than not with those women. We each longed for the same things: to care for our families, love our children well, be fed, clothed, housed, and feel safe. And once those basic needs were met, we all longed to be a part of something meaningful and use our talents to live up to our potential. Personal growth and professional development are magical when they lead to human flourishing. But these women were just trying to survive. We saw so many women go from surviving to thriving in our Artisan Partner groups through Trades of Hope. They could now keep their babies, feed their families, create safe spaces, and contribute to their communities in real and tangible ways.

John F. Kennedy once said, "A rising tide lifts all ships." And Trades of Hope has become a rising tide for women. For this, I am very grateful that our hard work is helping women step up and out of poverty. And I'm passionate about the work we do because, the truth is, *no one rises alone*. Not me, not you, not any woman around us. We all rise *together*.

But I'd be remiss if I didn't say, *we've also got a long way to go*. As long as there are women still living in poverty, still being oppressed, abused, trafficked, forced to give up their babies due to a lack of food, and sending their young children off to work rather than to school—we have more work to do!

For anyone who wants to join our rising tide but feels overwhelmed by the work, here are four simple steps for you to *do what only you can do*, starting today:

1. Recognize the power you have with every dollar you spend.

When it comes to fair-trade fashion and ethical spending, the truth is in the statistics. According to Clutch, 75 percent of shoppers prefer to shop with a business that supports a social cause.[36] But I learned that we had to be personally passionate about our cause if we were going to convince others of the same. If I wanted women (and men) to understand the power of every dollar they spend, I had to be mindful of my power, too. This isn't me telling you *what* to buy and *where* to spend your money. It's me encouraging you to be aware of *how* you spend your money. Awareness is the first powerful step towards any kind of change in our lives.

Understanding the power to change the trajectory of women's lives in developing countries through job creation and ethical spending is what has kept us going at Trades of Hope for over 12 years. And it's taken a lot of perseverance, a strong commitment to our mission, and a consistent work ethic. We are relentless in our work to create opportunities for women to leave poverty and trafficking because *we are women, too.* As Elisabeth says,

"While we don't face the same harsh realities as most women around the world, we stand with them because we feel connected in our sisterhood. It feels personal. And I would encourage anyone trying to create a social impact to identify a cause that feels personal to them."

If all of us started tracking how we spend our money (even if we just tracked our fun or "extra" purchases such as accessories, gifts, etc.) and committed to making a 10% shift in how we spend, that slight shift could make a HUGE difference over time. So here's my encouragement to you: the next time you purchase a gift for your mom, your daughter, or your sister, *consider buying those $30 pair of earrings made by a person you know was fairly paid.* Your commitment to buying something ethically-made or locally-sourced when purchasing a gift for someone else is probably the 10% change you could easily make today.

2. Practice "slow fashion" when purchasing fashion and lifestyle accessories.

Eighty percent of people who make clothing in the fashion industry are women ages 18-24, and the majority of them make less than $3 a day.[37] These women have dreams for a better future. But many of these women have no other choice but to endure unsafe working conditions and unreasonable working hours, working 12–14-hour days, seven days a week, in factories for the sake of affordable fashion. They do this because most of these women have children who rely on their meager income for food, shelter, clothing, and schooling.

And the dangers are real. On April 24, 2013, a Bangladesh factory called Rana Complex collapsed, killing 1,134 garment workers and injuring over 2,500. Most of these workers were women. This incident is still considered one of the worst industrial tragedies in history, stemming from structural failure and unsafe working conditions. Several more subsequent accidents in the garment industry eventually caused a revolution to create awareness, raise questions, and ultimately bring about change in what we consider a "fast fashion" world. This revolution started with people aware of these incidents, but it continues with consumers, like you and me, caring about the people who make the clothing we buy.

You don't have to look far to realize the fashion industry has grown at a frenzied pace in the past few decades. Consumers crave the newest, hottest, fresh-off-the-runway styles. This "fast fashion" focuses on quick, cheap production. Manufacturers underbid their competitors to keep up with consumers' demand to buy clothing for less than $20 apiece. When issues arise at fashion factories—issues such as large cracks in the foundation or walls or other structural warning signs—the pressure to meet these industry demands doesn't allow for downtime to address unsafe working conditions. As a result, fashion companies and their factories operating without accountability often choose risk over human rights.

This is why we're committed to "slow fashion" and fair-trade practices at Trades of Hope. We want women to have opportunities to work in safe environments and make living wages within reasonable hours. This leads to slower production times and yet should be a priority to any product-based business that wants to help others. If we want to invest in the well-being and health of women, and in the sustainability of their communities, then slow production is the fair trade we're willing to make. This is also why we pay our Artisan partners their asking price up-front, so our discounts and sales to customers never affect their income. It's why we offer training and educational opportunities for their personal growth. It's also the reason why we know the names, stories, struggles, and dreams of our women, along with their desires to meet their full potential. We all stand shoulder to shoulder as equals—Artisan Partners, US Partners, our home office team, and the women who purchase our products. Together, we are ALL worthy of the opportunity to live a beautiful life.

One more thing I want you, the empowered consumer, to know is that ethically-made fair-trade fashion isn't just about safe working conditions and livable wages. *It's also about corporate and social responsibility.* Fair-trade accountability also requires companies to be mindful of things such as fabric dyes (*how toxic are the dyes?*) and leather tanning (*how natural are the tannins used?*). The fashion industry has made a lot of strides, and we've come a long way with how we consume fashionable goods. But I'm still shocked at how manufacturers are treated when there are no outside views or accountable measures for industry business practices. If a company isn't willing to share information regarding their factory conditions or how their workers are treated, then it's safe to assume they are prioritizing profit margins over people. So, as you shift 10% of your purchases, make sure those purchases come with fair-trade certification, Fair Trade Federation (FTF) membership, B-Corp status, or provide proof of factory certification required by socially responsible fashion companies.

If more consumers like you and me start asking questions, demanding answers, and making choices based on company responses, our spending power benefits every single person involved in making the products we purchase. Another example of the rising tide.

3. Choose sustainable development over charitable bandaids.

Any person or company can throw money at a cause and call it good. But the lasting impact goes beyond monetary transactions. As I've said before, charity is necessary for relief aid and humanitarian crises. But long-term, sustainable development is required to change the tide of generational poverty. That's why we invest in our Artisans' education, business development, personal growth—and at the end of the day—our relationship. To see Artisan Partners thrive, we create jobs through purchase orders with Artisan communities so women can support themselves. When necessary, we make additional investments to help these women better their lives. Those additional investments include adult literacy classes, professional development (from how to read tech packs to how to create quality control procedures), and health and wellness programs. How we measure our social impact goes beyond finances. We support our Artisan Partners as they develop skills that will serve them for the rest of their lives. This gives them something charitable donations cannot: *dignity and pride.*

Of course, as we've already mentioned, there are times when we participate in charitable giving, too. But most of our charitable giving goes to support the development already happening in the Artisan communities. When Artisan Partners call or email to say they're in need of sewing machines to expand product lines and hire more female Artisans, vans to safely transport rescued human trafficking survivors, or more orders during global economic crisis, we do what we can to invest in these needs.

4. Join us at Trades of Hope to support more job creation and amplify the voices of women around the world.

I hear a lot of women talking about how hard it is to find work with a company or organization they completely trust. A recent study found that "ethical drivers are 3x more important to company trust than competence." Meaning employees care more about whether or not they work for a trustworthy company regardless of how well the company does what they do.[38] The study also highlights how more Americans are doing research to see if a company is being authentic when they take a stand on a particular issue. This means companies like Trades of Hope can talk about ethically-made fair-trade fashion, but our consumers are doing their homework to see if our actions live up to what we say. And the good thing about us is that they do! Our actions and our words are the same.

So, if you're looking to supplement your income so you can increase your grocery budget, build a better college fund for your kids, or take that vacation you've dreamed of, then the best-case scenario is when you can trust the company and use your career to champion the causes most important to you. And if women helping other women lead their families out of poverty is a passion of yours, we'd love to have you join our team at Trades of Hope!

When you sell or purchase pieces from our exclusive line of ethically-made fair-trade fashion and home accessories, it increases the demand for products made by women in need around the world. By shopping styles made by our Artisan Partners, these women are acknowledged for their valuable presence in the world and given a platform to use their voices. With every product sold through a home party in the US, job opportunities increase for thousands of Artisan Partners around the world. And we couldn't do it without our amazing customers, hostesses, and partners—all women just like you and me.

What I love about our business model is that our Partners in the US also have the opportunity to earn a fair wage, participate in training and support for their businesses, and grow and develop as a person *and* as a professional. Most of our Partners would say it was the *mission* of Trades of Hope that brought them in, the fun *events* and the *paycheck* that kept them engaged, and the *rising tide* of our global sisterhood that makes them lifelong fans of the work happening in Artisan communities around the world. Not to mention, the fair-trade products we sell on behalf of our Artisan Partners help women look fashionable and feel beautiful! Whether you're a college student, a young entrepreneur, a stay-at-home mom, or a seasoned business professional, who doesn't want to *look* good and *do* good?! We've also worked hard over the years with our Artisan Partners to improve the quality of these goods without drastically raising prices for our customers so that these pieces will last longer in closets. This is one of the many ways the cycle of sustainability goes both ways at Trades of Hope. Our ethically-made fair-trade products mean sustainable jobs for women coming out of poverty, and they mean longer-lasting wardrobe pieces for more sustainable fashion.

Becoming a Partner with Trades of Hope is a simple step toward making a global impact with every dollar you and your friends spend.

CHANGING MINDSETS

Because I grew up with a scrappy mom who was a great bargain shopper, I also loved hunting to get the most products at the lowest price. More was better. And it was fun! I loved seeing how many great pieces we could find on sale racks at Hudson's. And when I got home, how many outfits I could make from my new pieces (after all, this is how I won the "best dressed" award as a high school senior!) But this is such an American mindset—that it's better to have five inexpensive pairs of jeans than one pair that costs a little more. It's a mindset of *more for less*.

But ethically-made fair-trade fashion is *less for more*. And that's what I hope we are willing to see as a society. I never really knew if what I was buying applied fair-trade practices to their fashionable jeans or sweaters. I didn't care about those things as a teenager. I didn't even know to care about these things in my 30s. But like so many other people, I always cared about the images of starving mothers and children in commercials on my parents' TV screen. And now, I have enough knowledge to connect the dots between those women and children and the way I spend money on my end.

When we know better, we do better.

It's important to pause and share something I know to be true: I realize that there are so many women trying to scrape by on sale racks and discount stores just to provide for their families. Please hear me when I say that *I do not judge how you spend your money or where you spend it*. My hope is only that we all do better when possible.

Another mindset I had to change on my journey towards ethical spending through fair-trade fashion is something that goes beyond the wallet. As a grown woman, I realized that every time I felt insecure about myself, I thought I could find my confidence in a new piece of clothing. If my weight fluctuated and left me feeling "blah" about myself, *I bought a new piece of clothing.* If I was asked to speak at an event that seemed "out of my league," *I bought a new piece of clothing.* If Frits and I decided to take a warm weather vacation somewhere, and I wasn't crazy about the idea of being in a bathing suit around beautiful, tanned-skin people, *I bought a new piece of clothing.* You get the idea, and I'm sure you could fill in your own sentences here about the things you've purchased in moments when you felt insecure, too. The change for me happened when I was willing to stand in front of my closet with "new eyes." I already had everything I needed to show up in a new situation and look beautiful and fashionable. I just needed to dig deep to regain my confidence. Now when I feel insecure, instead of buying new clothes, I lean in and get curious about why I feel the way I do. Then I pull something out of my closet and trust that my feelings will follow the confidence I exude in what I choose to wear that day.

When it comes to changing our mindsets, *awareness* is the start of everything. But real-life change happens when we're willing to *take action.*

ENDLESS POSSIBILITIES

The sky's the limit at Trades of Hope. As long as poverty exists, there will be plenty of opportunities for you to be a part of helping us create jobs for women. In doing so, we are actively working together toward alleviating poverty and human trafficking.

In early 2022, as previously mentioned, Elisabeth and I started a podcast called *Legacy.* It has become the place where we challenge women to find their purpose, live intentionally, and act with passion. Whether it's joining the work we're doing at Trades of Hope or stepping into another calling, our hope is to encourage all of us as women to be unapologetically our best selves. Being the best version of ourselves isn't solely for our own benefit. It allows us to help our sisters rise with us, too. When we lead intentional lives, boldly believing that we can make a difference, we can confidently use our voices and pursue our dreams. And the women watching us will feel permission to do the same. I believe we were all put on this earth to do big things for each other as we work to make our world a better place. But if we lack confidence in ourselves and allow a lot of negative self-talk, then we hold ourselves back from doing what we were meant to do.

Some of us need to hear that being confident isn't the same thing as being *self-centered*. This is some of the cultural baggage of being a mission-driven faith-filled female in the world today. As a result, I see so many women pouring into everyone around them except for themselves, and they're *exhausted!* Can you relate? Yet, having confidence in ourselves and our capabilities is what allows us to get out of our own way and really serve others. And isn't that what most of us want—*to live a meaningful life that serves and benefits others?* Elisabeth and I have worked with a lot of women over the years—Artisans, Partners, and other women purchasing our products—who wrestle with this idea of having confidence. That is until they realize how their ability to believe in themselves affects hundreds if not thousands of other women and their ability to be confident too.

My purpose in life is to make a better world for the global sisterhood of women, and my passion in doing so is helping women find jobs so they can provide for their families, alleviate poverty, and end human trafficking. For most, if not all, of us, developing a job skill and being educated about a particular service, product, or trade is what allows us to pass our confidence onto other women. That's why at Trades of Hope, our passion for job creation through fair-trade fashion allows our Artisan Partners, Partners, and people connected to our mission to use fashion as a force for good. It's about job creation for women. It's about giving women choices and helping them be the heroes of their own stories. It's about giving women the opportunity to provide for their children without having to rely on charities for the rest of their lives. In its simplest form, my why always comes back to this: I want mothers to be able to keep their children and care for their families well.

And for Elisabeth, while she cares deeply about helping to prevent poverty orphans and alleviating human trafficking, she also takes those ideas a few steps further to empower women to rise out of oppressive cultures so they can experience equality and opportunity through financial independence.

It makes my heart sing to see women do something they never thought possible. We're using *fashion as a force for good* in so many ways at Trades of Hope that if you showed the 20-year-old version of me what I'd be up to right now, I would have been so surprised! Never in my wildest dreams would I have imagined doing work that helps other women create such lasting change in their lives. And at Trades of Hope, we're all about women lifting up other women. We're all about making a difference and dreaming big.

And here are a few of my big dreams:

> *I dream of a world where every woman recognizes the power she has in how she spends her dollars.*
>
> *I dream of a world where people understand that business can be used as a force for good.*
>
> *I dream of a world where our Partners at Trades of Hope outnumber the crowds of women who show up for Fashion Week in Paris every year.*
>
> *I dream of a world where we help our Artisan Partner groups build schools in their communities.*

I dream of a world where people are not sold and used for financial gain.

I dream of a world where mothers don't abandon their children due to potential starvation.

I dream of a world where women rise together.

Running a direct sales company in a post-COVID world has challenged every ounce of those dreams, and yet it's still the passion that burns bright in my life and the lives of women like my daughter Elisabeth, our leadership team, our Partners, and Artisan Partners.

Of course, I'd love to invite you into our dream—for your dream to be our dream, too. But only you know what your dreams are and what it will take for you to live out those dreams. If nothing else, consider:

What are the dreams you have for yourself? And then, what dreams do you have for the world around you?

I spend a lot of time thinking about how we can make the impossible possible for women living in poverty. And every day, I ask myself one question as it relates to my purpose and my passion:

"How can I help women keep their children, alleviate poverty, and human trafficking in the world?"

The answer I keep coming back to is the work we're doing at Trades of Hope. This is what it means to be a rising tide of voices.

"A rising tide lifts all the ships."
–Kennedy

TRADES OF HOPE TIMELINE

2010—The start of Trades of Hope, our first season of home parties and fair-trade product testing. We sold $27,000 in our first four months and were thrilled!

2011—We went to Haiti to meet Artisans for Trades of Hope. We were packaging and shipping from storage units. Our first group of sales consultants included Cori Salgado and Linda Jenkins, and our first team members outside of the four of us: Katelyn Spina and Stacy Barksdale. The search continued for more global Artisan Partners.

2012—We moved into a real office with a distribution center at the back of a church's coffee shop. We continued growing our sales, connections and establishing relationships with Artisan Partners in more countries.

2013—Trades of Hope sales were growing at 400% year over year. We were working with more Artisan Partners and adding new product lines. Melissa Powell joined our team. (We hit the jackpot with 99% of our home office hires, especially with Melissa.) We took Partners on the first of many trips to Haiti to visit Artisans.

2014—Julie McKay joined our team for product development/ design and strengthened Artisan Partnerships. We held the first annual convention, which we now call Inspire.

2015—Gretchen went to Cambodia and met Ya.

2016—Stacie Beck joined our team as Head of Partner Development. Elisabeth and Gretchen traveled to Peru to meet with Artisan groups.

2017—We hired our first COO, Jeremy Cundiff. Lucas Caldeira joins our team and oversees Artisan Partner group relationships from India. We added more groups of Artisans from more countries and grew the year's annual sales to over $12 million.

2018—Michelle Cundiff (my longtime friend involved with Three Angels) joined our team to plan events like Inspire. Co-founders transitioned from four to two, with Gretchen and Elisabeth remaining. We went to Africa for the first time to meet with groups in Kenya and Uganda.

2019—Haitian Artisans helped host Inspire. We took Partners to Guatemala to visit four Artisan groups for the first time.

2020—In January, Gretchen and Elisabeth went to meet with Artisans in Thailand. When COVID-19 hit, we paused home parties, encouraged women to purchase our products online, and they were amazing. We placed orders when other companies were canceling them.

2021—Elisabeth completed her master's degree in Strategic Communications for Social Change and became CBO (Chief Brand Officer). Gretchen and Elisabeth were featured in Forbes.

2022 + beyond— We did something I said we would never do and bought a building for Trades of Hope in Florida to enjoy as we boldly step into the future together.

ACKNOWLEDGEMENTS TO PARTNERS

....

To the thousands of amazing Partners (women and men) who have sold Trades of Hope products over the past 12 years, to say "thank you" is not nearly enough. We are incredibly grateful to you for helping us build this missional business to positively impact women and children all around the world. More mothers have been able to keep their children safe and close to them and send them to school because you have spread the word about the products they have created.

Many of you have worked so hard to build your independent businesses and Trades of Hope overall. You have been a gift to know and work beside over the years. Countless names and faces come to mind, and there is no way that I could mention everyone. But there is one woman who has been with us as a Partner since the beginning. She has been a strong presence, a top seller, and a gift to us as leaders in this company. I want to give a huge "thank you" to Linda Jenkins. We are blessed to have you in this sisterhood and appreciate your tenacity.

To our current Directors within Trades of Hope: Jess Argetsinger, Erin Woods, Melanie Sunukjian, Melissa Patchett, Dawn Hansen, Shelby Black-Couch, Susan Johnston, Spring Mingey, Jocelyn Doese, Jamie Driggers, and Veronica Martinez, thank you for your heartfelt, passionate leadership. You help make this sisterhood great every single day!

Thank you to the women who sell thousands of our pieces each year or a few pieces each month. *Together* we get to further our impact and provide more opportunities to Artisan Partners, mostly women, and their children around the world. I hope that your partnership with Trades of Hope fills you up in a multitude of ways every day. I love working with you!

I'm so looking forward to all of the years to come as we see more women rise together.

A NOTE TO OUR PARTNERS & CUSTOMERS

Before Trades of Hope, I (Gretchen) was a mother of two young children when I began looking into international adoption. Our life was great, and I was grateful. But I felt a restlessness knowing most people around the world weren't as blessed as we were.

Have you ever felt that way?

A little nudge in the pit of your stomach? Deep down, I knew I had to do something. Without knowing where it was on a map yet, I went on a trip to Haiti and was shaken by the corruption of many orphanages there.

I couldn't un-see what I saw, and I knew that staying silent in the face of injustice was complicit. So, without any prior experience, I started and ran an orphanage in Port-au-Prince for almost a decade. During that time, we helped 100 children find forever families. I knew in my head that it was a good thing. Adoption is a beautiful act.

But one truth kept tugging at my heart...

More often than not, the children given to our care had living parents, grandparents, or relatives. These parents loved their children but couldn't afford to feed them. They were desperate. There were too many tears and heartbreaking goodbyes. It felt so unjust to me.

In 2010, I teamed up with my daughter Elisabeth and our friends Holly and Chelsie to create jobs for mothers around the world so that they could keep their babies. The four of us started Trades of Hope to empower women. But you all—our ethical shoppers, party hostesses, and Partners ...

...you all turned it into a MOVEMENT of HOPE.

When you **shop our pieces**, our Artisans do a happy dance because we can place more orders. (Literally, they've sent us videos!) When you **host an event**, the purchases your friends make create more jobs for more women who just want an opportunity.

When you **join our accepting sisterhood** of Partners, you stand in solidarity with women around the world, shake their hands, and enter a dignified partnership where you rely on each other to bless your families and chase your dreams.

You are the link in this story that can give purpose to a bracelet, opportunity to a mother, and hope to the world. I'm so glad our stories have crossed. Because we started Trades of Hope for women around the world, but

We started it for you, too.

Light and love,

Gretchen

"After seeing the shortcomings of charity,
I love creating jobs so more women
can take care of their children
and thrive themselves.
I feel so grateful for this movement
and the hope we've inspired."

–GRETCHEN HUIJSKENS
FOUNDER AND CEO

5 POSTURES OF SUCCESSFUL WOMEN

From Legacy: A podcast for visionary women.

1. **Own your own stuff.** Women who are truly successful at whatever they're doing have one thing in common—they own their own stuff . . . the good, the bad, the ugly. Scrappy determination is what encompasses all of this. Don't wait around and expect other people to do it for you . . . just own your stuff and get it done.

2. **Don't claim defeat because of what someone else has done to you or didn't do for you.** I've seen a lot of women try to be successful in other areas, but as soon as people start blaming or not living up to expectations, there's a victim mentality—which isn't helpful. We are responsible for figuring out how to make it happen. Be willing to do the little things. These are the important building blocks (answering emails, going to meetings, grabbing groceries, following up with leads, customers, and network connections). Be willing to do these tasks every day to get to where you want to go. It's easy to procrastinate when it doesn't feel important. Keep the big picture in the forefront of your mind. "You don't rise to the level of your goals, you fall to the level of your systems."[39]

3. **Surrounding yourself with great people.** I once heard someone say, "You become like the five people you spend the most time with." Have good people around you that hold you to a certain standard of believing the best about others. My best girlfriends listen to me complain and then ask, "So what are you going to do about it?" When I get to the office and I'm talking to our employees, I'm mindful of what kind of conversation I'm bringing up. We would love to be around intelligent, capable people all of the time, but we need others

to feed into us. Who you spend your time with matters! And what you listen to, read, and watch affects your inner and outer self.

4.   **Have an intentional relationship with yourself.** I caught myself writing something one day and saying out loud, "That's so dumb, Gretchen!" Then I caught myself again and thought, "Would I say that to Elisabeth? Or one of the women we work with? Then why would I say it to me? What's the benefit?" We need to give ourselves what we'd be willing to do or give to our kids or best friends: affirmations and positive, constructive feedback.

5.   **Have a growth mindset.** We all need to believe in our own abilities. These abilities can be developed with hard work, confidence, and perseverance. "Confidence is not a feeling, it's a choice," says Elisabeth.

AUTHOR BIO

....

Gretchen Huijskens is co-founder and CEO of Trades of Hope, an ethical fashion company that empowers women out of poverty. Trades of Hope exists to create jobs for women in communities of extreme poverty by selling an exclusive line of high-quality, fair-trade accessories made by Artisan Partners around the world. Trades of Hope, which started in 2010, champions Fashion as a Force for Good.™ Motivated to create jobs for mothers so they don't have to give up their babies to orphanages, Gretchen helps women rise out of poverty, trafficking, and gender inequality by selling their fair-trade goods with the support of women across the US, called Trades of Hope Partners. She is a pioneer in the field of sustainable business, and the partnerships she creates empower every single woman involved around the world.

Before Trades of Hope, Gretchen founded an orphanage, a school, and a medical clinic in Haiti. Her experiences on the ground showed her how charity sometimes perpetuated a problem in developing countries, but business could be used to solve problems and create sustainable social impact. Gretchen has channeled her passion and expertise into growing Trades of Hope into a multi-million dollar company that reaches thousands of people around the world.

Gretchen and her team now work with thousands of Trades of Hope Partners in the US, selling fair-trade fashion and accessories made by Artisan Partners in over 15 countries worldwide.

Endnotes

· · · · · · · · · ·

Chapter One: Shaken and Stirred

1. https://www.britannica.com/event/2010-Haiti-earthquake
2. https://www.kqed.org/quest/5016/what-went-wrong-with-the-buildings-in-haiti
3. http://content.time.com/time/specials/packages/article/0,28804,1953379_1953494_1957885,00.html
4. http://content.time.com/time/specials/packages/article/0,28804,1953379_1953494_1957885,00.html
5. Some names have been changed to protect people's identities
6. Some names have been changed to protect people's identities
7. TIME Magazine: How NASCAR Came to the Rescue of Haiti Orphans (January 30, 2010)
8. https://www.uscis.gov/humanitarian/humanitarianpublicbenefitparoleindividualsoutsideUS
9. Some names have been changed to protect people's identities

Chapter Two: Wise Instincts

10. https://www.semesteratsea.org/field-programs/missionaries-charity-center-sp18/
11. https://www.biblegateway.com/passage/?search=Matthew%2025%3A45&version=NLT

Chapter Three: Hopeful Charity

12. https://restavekfreedom.org
13. https://en.wikipedia.org/wiki/Cit%C3%A9_Soleil
14. https://www.biblegateway.com/passage/?search=1+Samuel+7%3A12&version=NLT
15. https://www.usaid.gov/sites/default/files/documents/1862/USAID_Haiti_Education_Fact_Sheet_-_January_2020.pdf
16. https://www.amazon.com/When-Helping-Hurts-Alleviate-Yourself/dp/0802409989

Chapter Four: Navigating Change

17. Some names have been changed to protect people's identities

Chapter Five: Embracing Failure

18. https://bookshop.org/books/banker-to-the-poor-micro-lending-and-the-battle-against-world-poverty-2003-corr-2nd-printing/9781586481988

Chapter Six: Beginning Again

19. An expat is a person who lives outside their native country.
20. CARE Australia
21. https://www.tenthousandvillages.com/
22. https://en.wikipedia.org/wiki/Ten_Thousand_Villages
23. https://www.additudemag.com/slideshows/add-vs-adhd/
24. https://www.webmd.com/add-adhd/adhd-dyslexia-tell-apart
25. James 1:27 NIV Translation

Chapter Seven: Testing Your Theories

26. https://www.fairtradefederation.org/fair-trade-federation-principles/
27. Original author unknown

Chapter Eight: Imagining Opportunities

28. https://www.lowestwagechallenge.com/about-us
29. https://www.merriam-webster.com/dictionary/manifesto
30. DSEF Trades of Hope Case Study
31. https://www.nutriset.fr/products/en/plumpy-nut
32. CARE Australia

Chapter Nine: Searching for Partners

33. https://www.forbes.com/sites/Monicaburns/2021/08/01/
    got-goals-time-to-get-a-coach/?sh=11def13f3c2b
34. 2017 Trades of Hope Impact Report
35. Seth Godin talk on The History of Marketing

Chapter Ten: The Rising Tide

36. https://clutch.co/pr-firms/resources/
    how-corporate-social-responsibility-influences-buying-decisions
37. https://www.forbes.com/sites/quora/2017/07/26/
    fast-fashion-is-a-disaster-for-women-and-the-environment/?sh=587274811fa4
38. Porter-Navelli of Edelman's 2020 Trust Barometer

Conclusion

39. Quote by Author James Clear, *Atomic Habits*

Made in United States
North Haven, CT
19 June 2023

37867864R00128